ASPIRE

150
PROJECTS
TO GET YOU INTO THE
CULINARY
ARTS

ASPIRE

150

PROJECTS

TO GET YOU INTO THE

CULINARY
ARTS

Mark William Allison

BARRON'S

First edition for North America published in 2011 by
Barron's Educational Series, Inc.

A QUARTO BOOK

All inquiries should be addressed to:
Barron's Educational Series, Inc.
250 Wireless Boulevard
Hauppauge, New York 11788
www.barronseduc.com

ISBN-13: 978-0-7641-4671-8
ISBN-10: 0-7641-4671-8

Library of Congress Control Number: 2010931489

Conceived, designed, and produced by
Quarto Publishing plc
The Old Brewery
6 Blundell Street
London N7 9BH

Project manager: Cathy Meeus
Copy editor: Jo Godfrey Wood
Art director: Caroline Guest
Art editor: Hugh Schermuly
Designers: Steve Woosnam-Savage, Lee Riches
Picture research: Sarah Bell
Proofreader: Claire Waite Brown
Indexer: Dorothy Frame
Creative director: Moira Clinch
Publisher: Paul Carslake

Color separation by Pica Digital Pte Ltd , Singapore
Printed in Singapore by Star Standard Pte Ltd.

10 9 8 7 6 5 4 3 2 1

Dedication
My wife, Alison and my sons Jonathan, Matthew, and James

Contents

Chapter 3 **Meat, poultry, fish, & shellfish**

Chapter 4 **Vegetables, fruits, grains, & dried goods**

Chapter 5 **Dairy**

Chapter 6 **Baking**

Foreword

When I was at school, I enjoyed home economics, which consisted, at the time, of ironing, needlecraft, and, my favorite, cooking. My mother, along with my home economics teacher, Mrs. Grainger, brought out my talent and encouraged me to become a chef, advising me to go to culinary school. Thirty-one years later, I am now the dean of culinary education at one of the most prestigious culinary schools in the world, Johnson & Wales University. I oversee a college with 36 chef instructors and over 1,400 culinary students. Looking back, I have never been out of work and have traveled around the globe in my profession. I can honestly say I have enjoyed every minute. As a chef, you can be anywhere in the world and pick up a job. Forget the language barrier; food is its own universal language. Everyone loves to eat, and cooking is the easiest way that I know of to make lifelong friends.

I wish I had had a book like this when I was just starting out, a book that was easy to read and had pictures and illustrations of how to boil an egg and whip up cream, or information on different stoves and equipment used in a commercial kitchen. I remember buying two books for college, one for practical and one for theory. Both were over 400 pages long with few or no photographs, filled with French words that were difficult to pronounce and recipes that explained no real techniques. This book is a starting point for any aspiring chef. It will show you the basics that you need to know before ever stepping into class at a culinary school or starting work in a professional kitchen.

This is a step-by-step instructional book that shows you how to carry out culinary tasks using easy-to-follow workouts. Start at the beginning and work your way through to the end and you will have the first building blocks to becoming a great chef. Even if you already know the basics, I'm sure you will find this book interesting and inspiring. It will certainly help you with your studies at college or in the workplace.

Lastly, I tell my students "success is easy"–know what you want, work hard, and be consistent. You know what you want, as you have this book in your hands; that's the simple part. Now work hard and be consistent as you work your way through each and every workout. Practice will bring you success, but it's only the beginning of the truly wonderful experience of being a chef.

Keep cooking!

Mark William Allison

Getting started

To master the craft of culinary arts you need a thorough grounding in the basics. This means knowing about the setup of the kitchen and dining room brigade, menu planning, making recipes, ensuring food safety, and giving every recipe you make nutritional value. You need to know why you must have a good mixture of proteins, carbohydrates, and fats at each serving. You also need to know how heat affects the structure of food while it cooks and what temperatures are safe for it to be cooked to, and stored at, to avoid food poisoning and cross-contamination. In sum, you need to take care while storing, preparing, and cooking food, otherwise these things could cause you and your establishment trouble, and perhaps even make customers ill.

As an aspiring chef you also need to know the basic tools of the trade to accomplish the job at hand. You will learn the best knives to choose, the correct way to hold them, and how to keep them sharp and in their best condition. Also you will learn what the basic equipment requirements are in any kitchen and all the information you need to spot the difference between a pot and a pan or a flat-top stove and a stove with burners. So start now and remember that this is a learning process: if you make a mistake, just try again, take your time, and enjoy the workouts on every page.

The kitchen brigade

Georges-Auguste Escoffier (1847-1935) was considered the greatest chef of his time and is still revered by culinarians all over the world as the father of twentieth-century cookery. One of the main contributions that Escoffier made was to streamline the workplace and introduce the "brigade" system. This removed the chaos of the kitchen and established clear-cut responsibilities for each member of the team.

Chef

The word "chef" comes from the Latin "caput" and is the abbreviated form of the French phrase chef de cuisine, meaning "chief" or "head" of a kitchen. Today the term "chef" usually refers to the person in charge of the kitchen.

Teamwork
When you are working in the kitchen you must be prepared to be part of the team. This is particularly important at busy times.

Who's who in the kitchen

The kitchen brigade consists of a range of defined roles, from the most senior, the chef, to the most junior, the commis chef. Working their individual stations in the kitchen, together they create a smooth-running team.

Executive chef, or **chef de cuisine** (*shef deh kwih-ZEEN*). This person is responsible for all aspects of food production, menu-planning, hiring and training of staff, and budget.

Sous chef (*soo shef*). The term "sous" in French means "under"; the assistant to the executive chef or chef de cuisine. His or her main responsibilities include the scheduling of the kitchen team and the general day-to-day operations involved in food production.

Chef de partie (*shef deh pahr-TEE*), or station chefs, are in charge of particular areas. The following are the most important station chefs:

Saucier (*so-see-ay*). This position is considered the highest station in the kitchen, under the executive chef and sous chef. The saucier is in charge of all sautéed foods and their sauces.

Poissonier (*pwah-so-nyay*) fabricates fish and shellfish and prepares fish and shellfish dishes. Depending on the size of the kitchen, this position may be the responsibility of the saucier.

Rotisseur (*ro-tee-sur*), or roast chef, and **grillardin** (*gree-ar-dan*), or grill chef, are in charge of roasts and grilled items on the menu. Depending on the size of the kitchen, these jobs may be combined.

Entremetier (*awn-truh-met-yay*), the vegetable chef, is responsible for all the starches on the menu, including the vegetables, soups, pasta, and egg dishes.

Garde manger (*gard-mawn-shay*) is the cold production chef, whose jobs include such things as preparing salads and dressings, cold appetizers, pâtés, and all the buffet items. The garde manger may also fabricate meats and fish.

Patissier (*pa-tees-syay*), or pastry chef, makes all the pastries and desserts and may also prepare the bread items.

Expediter, or **aboyeur** (*ah-bwa-yer*), accepts the orders from the waiters and relays them to the chefs in each station. He/she is usually the last person to see the finished dish leave the kitchen.

Commis (*koh MEE*) **chef**, or apprentice cook, works with the station chefs to learn how the station operates.

 1 Workout: Try the basics

Get to know the basics first. Like any area of expertise, you need to master first principles before you can progress to the very top. Starting today, read this book from cover to cover and try out each and every workout. With this experience under your belt, the fun can really begin; the basic skills you have acquired are the essential building blocks, leading to a fulfilling and exciting life as a professional chef.

Front of house

Just as the kitchen has its brigade, the front of house (or dining room) also needs a line of management, the dining room brigade.

Maître d'hôtel (*may-truh-doh-tell*). Similar to the executive chef or chef de cuisine, the maître d'hôtel is the person ultimately in charge of the running of the dining room. He or she works very closely with the executive chef to determine the menu and wine selection. The job also involves hiring and training staff and organizing seating.

Sommelier (*se mel yay*), or wine steward, is responsible for all aspects of the wine service, from preparing a wine list, to purchasing wines, beers, and liquors, to assisting guests in their choice of the best wine pairing for their meal.

Chef de salle (*shef duh sal*), or the head waiter, will generally be in charge of the running of service during operation hours.

Chef d'étage (*shef day tahj*), or captain, shows the guests to their seats, explains the menu, and takes the customers' order at the same time as answering any questions about the menu. He or she will also prepare any table side dishes, if required.

Chef de rang (*shef duh rhang*), or front waiter, sets the table and may rearrange it depending on what the guests have chosen. He or she will deliver the food and take care of any needs the guests may have, promptly and courteously.

Commis de rang (*koh MEE duh rhang*), just like the commis chef, this position is generally the most junior of the front of house. The commis will learn how to set up tables, fill water glasses, remove the plates between courses, and assist the chef d'étage and chef de rang before and during the service.

2 Workout: Scrapbook

Build up your own scrapbook or collection of recipes you have saved from magazines and newspapers—it's a great way to learn new things and it's fun to create a book that you can keep forever. Clip the recipes you like the sound of and try out a new one at least once a week. Your personal collection of recipes will keep you supplied with a never-ending resource of new ideas. You can purchase ready-made albums to paste your finds into or slot them into ready-made pockets.

Chain of command
At busy times the front of house personnel must work as a closely connected team in order to deliver the excellent service that diners expect.

3 Workout: Bookstores

Spend time in bookstores researching culinary techniques, recipes, and cooking methods, but resist the temptation to buy too many books at once. Save your money, then buy one that you know you are going to use, read it from cover to cover, and try out ideas, before going out to buy another.

4 Workout: Homework

Do your homework—nobody becomes the best at anything without putting serious time in. You have read about the brigade system of the kitchen and front of house; now learn the name of each section by heart. Then be prepared to work each section in turn until you reach the top of the brigade system; that's what it takes to become the best.

How to build a menu

A menu is a list of dishes served at a restaurant, to give the customer a choice of what to eat and a description of the flavors to expect.

For the restaurateur the menu is the most important document in the business. It reflects sales, food production, accounting, purchasing, the labor needed to produce and serve the food, the layout of the kitchen, and equipment needed to produce the menu satisfactorily.

The menu

Whether you intend to work in a fine-dining restaurant, a mom-and-pop restaurant, or a hamburger-chain restaurant, you will soon discover that the menu, combined with good food and good service, helps ensure success.

Most menus offer enough choice to build an entire meal; a typical menu will offer three courses. The first course is the starter, which may be hot or cold. These include appetizers, salads, and soups. The main course, or entrée, comes second and usually includes protein, which could be meat, poultry, fish, shellfish, tofu, or another vegetarian offering, along with a vegetable/salad and carbohydrates, such as rice or potatoes. It is important to offer a range of vegetarian and allergy-free options. The third course is dessert. Again, this can be hot or cold and can cover anything from ice creams, cakes, and pastries, to fruit or a selection of cheeses.

A more formal dinner menu will contain a progression of courses, with anything from three to 20 dishes, depending on the style of restaurant, size of portions, and the type of food served. "Tasting menus" are becoming popular in top restaurants, offering small portions of a wide range of dishes.

Breakfast menu

A typical breakfast menu will include a selection of fruits, juices, cereals, breads, and hot items such as bacon, eggs, pancakes, and waffles, with regional specialties.

Lunch menu

Usually lunch menus need to contain quick-service items, since many people may only have an hour in which to grab a bite to eat. Sandwiches, soups, and salads are good choices for lunch menus because they are quick and easy to make and serve. However, you still need to offer variety, since you want repeat business and customers who regularly eat at your restaurant require a good selection of items to choose from.

Dinner menu

Dinner may be the main meal of the day, so this menu should contain a good choice of dishes that appeal to customers, served in a relaxed, friendly environment.

Putting a menu together

The chef has important input to the menu, but creating a successful one that sells well requires the input of many. The style of the cover, the artwork, layout, color, paper, and typeface all need to be considered by the chef, the management, designer, and marketing team.

Styles of menu

A "fixed," or "static," menu rarely changes from day to day. This style is usually offered at schools, colleges, or in fast-food chains, ethnic restaurants, and in franchise restaurants.

A "cycle" menu has been developed to repeat itself over a certain timeframe. It could take the form of a different menu every day for seven days. However, every Saturday, for example, is the same as the Saturday before. This type of menu is good for hospitals, nursing homes, schools, and colleges. It could be a seasonal menu, which changes over the year (spring, summer, fall, and winter), offering customers the best-quality products in season at the best prices. This is great for privately owned restaurants and hotels.

A "market" menu really depends on what is available at the market on any given day, so the menu may change daily. Many top chefs like to use market menus because it gives them the challenge of coming up with new and interesting dishes, using fresh, seasonal products daily or weekly.

Menu language

Menus are normally offered in up to three categories:

1 **À la carte** means that everything, from food to beverages, is priced individually and ordered separately.

2 **Table d'hôte** usually offers customers a fixed choice of dishes and gives no selection other than what is on the menu.

3 **Fixed-price** offers the customer a selection of choices, but the cost of the whole meal is a fixed price.

Many restaurants these days offer a mixture of à la carte, table d'hote, and fixed-price menus to their customers, giving them a greater choice.

A modern menu

Course	Menu
First course	appetizer, soup, fish, salad
Main course	meat, poultry, fish, vegetarian option, vegetables, starches, salads
Dessert	pastries, cakes, fruits, cheese, selection of ice creams

The description of the dishes, how they are prepared, statements about quantity, quality, grade, and freshness are important information that must be on the menu. For example, if you are serving fresh Angus beef, then it must be Angus beef, and it needs to be fresh, not frozen. If the establishment boasts "freshly made, home-made desserts," then desserts have to be freshly made and created on the premises.

Descriptions such as "light," "healthy," and "heart-healthy" need to be backed with reliable data. Food safety laws also dictate that customers are made aware that certain foods need to be cooked to a certain temperature, unless otherwise requested. Statements such as "Consuming raw or undercooked meats, poultry, seafood, shellfish, or eggs may increase your risk of food-borne illness" need to be displayed on the menu. There must also be warnings if nuts are included, to protect those allergic to them.

5 Workout: Aspiring chef

As an aspiring chef, you need to eat out as much as possible and try different restaurants and cuisines. You can only become an accomplished chef by developing your tastebuds and finding out what ingredients go well together; all of this can be accomplished by trying new foods and different styles of cooking. Try to eat at a good-quality restaurant once a week, if you can afford it, or at the least once a month.

6 Workout: Make notes

When you are trying out new restaurants, take notes, or better still, ask if you can take the menu home. It's a good way to learn how to compose your own menus and it will give you plenty of new ideas.

7 Workout: Study presentation styles

Take photos of restaurant dishes before you dig into them; this will greatly help your plate presentation skills. Think of them as "works of art," which you can refer to quickly, whenever you need inspiration. Good plate presentation is very much an art form; it requires careful attention to colors, shapes, textures, and the arrangement of foods. This comes with practice and patience, but you can speed the process up by eating at great restaurants and picking up presentation tips from different chefs.

8 Workout: Market menu

Go shopping at the foodstore or, better still, at your local farmers' market. Decide to spend a small amount on a selection of groceries. Bring them home and design your own "market menu" for you, your family, and friends. You'll find this is a great way to learn new cooking methods and presentation skills on seasonal food items.

Menu-planning tips
- Do not repeat foods with the same, or similar, tastes or flavors.
- Do not repeat foods with the same texture or mouth-feel.
- Use as many varieties of color, shape, and texture as possible.
- Make menus balanced, with enough nutritional variety as possible.
- Know the limitations of the equipment and plan the menu accordingly.
- Know the limitations of the staff and offer items on the menu that they can easily prepare, cook, and serve to a high standard.

14 All about recipes

A recipe is a set of instructions giving the chef a list of ingredients, their amounts, and the way in which they are combined and cooked. The purpose of a recipe is to duplicate a dish exactly, each and every time it is made. A carefully designed recipe can streamline kitchen operations and also control costs.

A recipe, on its own, will not turn you into a great chef. It is learning basic kitchen principles and good techniques that will make you into a good, or great, chef. However, a recipe will certainly assist you. It all depends on how much time and energy you devote to developing your skills.

A "standardized" recipe, which is actually a customized recipe that is developed by an establishment for use in its own kitchen, by its own staff, using its own equipment, assumes that the chef has a certain knowledge that enables him or her to follow the instructions in the recipe and turn out a quality product. However,

Standardized recipe

A standardized recipe is made up of three separate components:
1. The type and amount of each ingredient.
2. The method of production and the detailed cooking procedure.
3. The number of portions and their size.

The following information may also be provided as part of the recipe:
• Name of the recipe.
• Ingredients and amounts, listed in the order in which they are used.
• Equipment needed.
• Simple directions for production of the dish.
• Preparations and cooking times.
• Portioning, plating, and garnishing.

if you don't know how to sauté or deep-fry a product first, then a standardized recipe won't tell you how to achieve that. Your judgment and experience are also required. The function of a standardized recipe is to control quality and quantity of the product, yield, and portion size.

Cookery books provide different instructions from standardized recipes. A cookery book recipe is an instructional recipe giving you the opportunity to practice techniques.

Achieving consistent product

When you are working in a professional setting, it is important to ensure that you turn out a consistent product each and every time you make it. This ensures quality, portion size, and efficient running of the kitchen. A recipe needs to be made the same way every time, no matter which chef makes it. Measurements in a kitchen may be made in three ways: by weight, by volume, or by count.

Weight

Weight is by far the best way to measure ingredients, because it gives the most accurate form of measurement. Using a good-quality set of scales is essential in your home kitchen and in the workplace.

Volume

Volume measurements are not as accurate as weighing measurements, but are far quicker to use, especially in a busy kitchen. Volume measurement uses cups, quarts, gallons, teaspoons, tablespoons, fluid ounces, and pints. Volume measurement is most commonly used to measure liquids.

Count

"Count" refers to the number of individual items that are used in the recipe. For example, you might need to use one chicken breast, four eggs, two fillets of Dover sole, and two lemons.

Common equivalents

Dash	⅛ teaspoon
3 teaspoons	1 tablespoon
2 tablespoons	1 fluid ounces
4 tablespoons	¼ cup (2 fluid ounces)
5 ½ tablespoons	⅓ cup (2 ⅔ fluid ounces)
16 tablespoons	1 cup (8 fluid ounces)
2 cups	1 pint (16 fluid ounces)
2 pints	1 quart (32 fluid ounces)
4 quarts	1 gallon (128 fluid ounces)
0.035 ounce (¹⁄₃₀ ounces)	1 gram
1 ounce	28.35 grams (rounded to 30 grams for convenience)
1 pound	454 grams
2.2 pounds	1 kilogram (1,000 grams)
1 teaspoon	5 millileters
1 tablespoon	15 millileters
1 fluid ounce	29.57 millileters (rounded to 30)
1 cup	0.24 liter
1 gallon	3.80 liters

Do not measure a recipe out in a mixure of imperial and metric. Use one system or the other, otherwise your recipe will not be accurate and the desired result will not be achieved.

9 Workout: Cooking for yourself and your family

To become a great chef you need to practice your skills every day and take every opportunity to cook for others, so that you can build confidence. One of the best, and most enjoyable, ways to do this is to cook for your family and friends. Make sure that you read the full recipe first, then gather your ingredients and measure them out correctly, whether by weight, volume, or count. You need to get to know your measurements. Also, it's vital to learn the different techniques and methods of cooking when you are using different ingredients.

10 Workout: Get your family involved

As you try different recipes and use new ingredients, get your family involved in asking you what ingredients work best in certain dishes. What cuts of meat work best in a braise or what will work best roasted and why? When are the products in season? Which food items marry well and which do not? This gets you to think on your feet and answer questions while you create new recipes. It will also help you retain more knowledge at the same time as perfecting your skills.

11 Workout: Collect cookery books

One of the best ways to hone your culinary skills is to read as many cookery books as possible and start your own collection. You can plunder secondhand bookstores and yard sales. Try recipes out several times over, until you have perfected each dish. Don't be afraid to match up ingredients that don't seem to go together. Fusion, not confusion, is the key: keep it simple but do experiment.

12 Workout: Cooking from a mystery box

Give your family or friends a modest amount of money and ask them to buy an assortment of mystery ingredients. Allocate yourself 30 minutes to look over the ingredients and come up with your own recipe, then make it and serve it. You'll be surprised at how creative you can be under pressure. It will also amaze your family and friends to see how talented and resourceful you can be with only a few ingredients and limited time.

The term is also used when the chef places orders with suppliers. However, you need to be aware that fruit and vegetables do not always weigh the same. For example, a 40-count of oranges might weigh 20 lb (9 kg), but a 30-count of oranges could also weigh 20 lb (9 kg), each individual piece of fruit being bigger.

The metric system is the easiest and most widely used form of measurement system in the world. The US (imperial) system is more difficult to use, because it uses pounds for weight and cups for volume. But to make it easier, both measurement systems are often used in cookery books. However, a standardized recipe will only give you the measurements used at that establishment (cups or grams, not both).

Using your skills

When you start to write your own recipes, you need to apply the techniques you have already learned. What are the basic cooking methods involved in your recipe? If it is roasting, then you need to know all the basic roasting procedures. What are the basic characteristics of the ingredients? Is the protein you have chosen to roast lean or fatty, tough, or tender? What are the functions of the ingredients? Do they add flavor, texture, or body to the recipe? What are the cooking times? Since cooking times vary from product to product, your judgment and experience will tell you if the product has reached the right temperature, texture, and degree of doneness.

Time yourself with a mystery box
Give yourself 30 minutes (see Workout 12) to look over the ingredients and come up with recipes and a menu.

Basics of nutrition

16

More and more people are becoming concerned about what they eat, so when planning your menus you need to have a basic understanding of what the body needs to function on a daily basis.

You will greatly benefit from knowing how energy and nutrients work together and how to develop healthy, flavorful, and satisfying menu dishes that are easy to prepare. The foundation of cooking is the understanding of ingredients, cooking techniques, and basic nutrition of food. All food has chemical compounds within it called "nutrients." it is these nutrients that supply our bodies with energy, regulate bodily functions, and replace and build body tissue. These nutrients can be broken down into categories: proteins, fats (lipids) and fiber, carbohydrates, vitamins, minerals, and water.

Proteins

Proteins consist of amino acids; these are the building blocks for body tissue, essential for growth and repair. The body can make most of the amino acids it needs, but there are some that it cannot make.

Food that contains all the essential amino acids are called "complete" proteins. Foods such as milk, meats, poultry, fish, and eggs contain complete proteins.

Other foods may be high in protein but do not carry all nine essential amino acids. These are called "incomplete" proteins. Nuts, grains, and beans are all good examples. You can still get all nine essential amino acids by eating from the different food groups in one sitting. These are called "complementary" proteins. The average adult needs about 1 ½ oz–2½ oz (45–75 g) of protein daily, but too much protein can lead to a variety of health problems, including kidney and liver damage.

Fats

Fats are good for you, since your body needs fat-soluble vitamins (A, D, E, and K) for proper bodily functions. Fats also supply the body with energy and are classified as "saturated," "monounsaturated," or "polyunsaturated." Saturated fats are solid at room temperature and come from animal products. Health experts believe that too much saturated fat in the diet can lead to heart disease and other health problems. Monounsaturated and polyunsaturated fats are liquid at room temperature; these fats are considered healthier than saturated fats. Monounsaturated fats are found in olive oil and canola oil, while polyunsaturated fats are found in corn oil and sunflower oil. Hydrogenated fats are changed from liquid to solid by adding hydrogen atoms to the fat molecules. These kinds of fats are called "trans" fats, and are unhealthy as they limit the body's ability to rid itself of cholesterol building up on artery walls. Too much fat of any kind is bad for your health.

Carbohydrates

Carbohydrates are compounds of carbon, hydrogen, and oxygen atoms bound together like chains. It is these chains that give the body its primary source of energy. The average person needs at least 1½–3½ oz (45–105 g) of carbohydrates per day. There are two kinds of carbohydrates: simple and complex. Simple carbohydrates (sugars) are found in table sugar and candy, while complex carbohydrates (starch combined with fiber) are found in whole grains, vegetables, and fruits. Many experts believe that

A balanced diet

If you consume a wide variety of foods while staying within your calorific needs, you are more likely to get all the nutrients your body needs. You need to eat from each of the groups daily. This means:
• At least four fruit servings.
• At least five vegetable servings.
• Three servings of whole grains.
• Three servings of fat-free or low-fat dairy products.

You may:
• Eat candy in moderation.
• Eat poultry and fish at least once per week.
• Eat red meats in moderation.
• Restrict total fat intake to 20–35 percent of daily calories.
• Consume less than one teaspoon of sodium per day.
• Drink alcoholic beverages in moderation; one drink per day for women and two drinks per day for men.

• You can maintain a healthy body weight by not consuming too many calories.
• If you engage in regular physical activity for at least 30 minutes every day you will burn off enough calories to keep your weight the same. Increase physical activity to 60–90 minutes if you need to lose weight.

Sources of nutrients

To stay healthy we must eat a varied diet, containing the essential nutrients. Selecting from each of the main food groups can create a balanced diet, containing all the vitamins and minerals the body needs.

Proteins   **Fats**   **Carbohydrates**   **Vitamins**   **Minerals**   **Water**

your diet should be made up of mainly complex carbohydrates, because these are released into the bloodstream more slowly than simple carbohydrates. What is more, the fiber they contain is very important for proper functioning of the intestinal tract.

Vitamins

Vitamins supply no energy, but are very important to the healthy functioning of the body. There are two types: water-soluble and fat-soluble. Vitamins B and C are water-soluble and need to be consumed every day, while fat-soluble vitamins, such as A, D, E, and K, can be stored in the body and do not need to be taken every day.

Minerals

Minerals fall into two groups: "major" minerals, including calcium, chloride, magnesium, sodium, and potassium, and "trace" minerals, which include copper, fluoride, iron, selenium, and zinc, among others. Minerals, just like vitamins, are essential for regulating certain bodily functions.

Water

Water makes up 50 to 60 percent of the body and plays a role in its every function, from digestion and waste removal to temperature control. The average adult should drink eight glasses of fluid daily.

Calories

A calorie is a unit of measurement of energy and is defined as the amount of heat needed to raise the temperature of 1000 g of water by 1°C at one atmosphere pressure.

⅓ oz (1 g) protein supplies four calories
⅓ oz (1 g) fat supplies nine calories
⅓ oz (1 g) carbohydrates supplies four calories

We all need to take more or less calories daily, depending on occupation and physicality, but there is a direct connection between calorie intake, physical activity, and weight gain. If you eat more calories than you burn, you gain weight. If you eat fewer calories than you burn, you lose.

What restaurants and chefs can do

Restaurants and chefs are becoming more concerned about people's health and are redefining their menus and cooking practices. They are also adding new, healthy items to their menus by:
• Using cooking techniques that use less fat, such as poaching, grilling, steaming, and baking.
• Using healthy oils such as olive and canola oil.
• Relying on natural flavors rather than adding salt, and adding more herbs and spices to the dishes.
• Using the freshest and highest-quality products available when in season.
• Storing food properly so that it doesn't lose its nutritional value.
• Reducing portion sizes.
• Putting more healthy choices on the menu.
• Offering main courses that emphasize plant instead of animal foods.
• Using nutritional information when compiling new menus.
• Pointing out healthy items on the menu to customers.
• Posting notices or labeling products that contain potential allergens on menus.

13 Workout: Making dishes healthier

Try making your own healthy hamburger. What can you change to make it healthier? Then get your family and friends to taste-test and see if your healthy alternative tastes as good as the less-healthy version. Hopefully it will taste better!

• Try using leaner cuts of meat such as ground chicken, turkey, or ostrich, which are all lower in saturated fat than beef.
• Grilling will reduce the amount of fat content in the burger compared with frying.
• Use low-fat instead of full-fat cheese.
• Top with fresh, raw vegetables such as lettuce, tomato, cucumber, and sliced onions.
• Swap the white bun for a tasty whole wheat bun, which is high in fiber.
• For your side of fries, rather than deep-frying, slice potatoes and lightly coat them in olive oil before baking them in the oven until crispy.

14 Workout: Creating a healthy three-course menu

Create a three-course menu following the healthy guidelines detailed in Workout 13. How can you reduce fat intake? By using leaner cuts of meat, using cooking techniques such as steaming, simmering, and grilling? How can you reduce the amount of animal protein in your menu? By using tofu or other meat substitutes? How can you use more vegetables and fruits creatively in your menu?

The next time you eat out, look at the menu and identify three of the most popular dishes served at the restaurant that use meat, fish, or poultry. At home, try to adapt those dishes for a vegetarian customer and see how easy, or hard, it is.

Food science

When food is heated it changes color, flavor, aroma, texture, and nutritional content. To be a skilled chef you need to know why these changes happen.

Cooked potatoes

Uncooked potatoes

How cooking alters food
Broiling, grilling, roasting, baking, sautéeing, pan-frying, and all the other methods give the food a specific texture, appearance, aroma, and flavor. Cooking affects the proteins, sugars, starches, water, and fats in the food in different ways.

Understanding the very basics of applying heat to food is essential when you become a chef. There are three ways in which heat is transferred to food: conduction, convection, and radiation.

Conduction
Conduction is the transfer of heat between two items as a result of direct physical contact and the inward movement of heat through the food. If you place a frying pan on the stove, the heat of the stove will transfer to the frying pan and the metal of the frying pan will conduct to the food, cooking it. Equipment that is best suited for conduction is made from copper and aluminum. Glass and porcelain are considered poor conductors of heat.

Induction units have glass or ceramic stove tops, which house electromagnetic energy coils underneath. These create an electrical current that penetrates the cooking equipment placed on it. This is a very rapid, efficient, and safe way to cook food. You need to use special induction cookware: copper, cast iron, or aluminum are not suitable for use on induction units.

Convection
Convection heat spreads through air and water, either naturally or mechanically. Natural convection happens when there is a circular movement in a liquid. If you place a pan of water on a stove, the water at the bottom of the pan heats up and rises to the surface. The cooler water at the top of the pan falls, creating a circular motion throughout the liquid, which eventually heats all the liquid in the saucepan. The natural circulation of heat is much slower

through thick liquids, so soups or sauces need to be stirred as they warm through, otherwise they may burn on the bottom of the pan. In addition, stirring helps to heat the food more rapidly and more evenly. Mechanical convection uses fans in convection ovens and convection steamers to quickly circulate hot air or hot water to evenly cook the food product.

Radiation
Radiation transfers energy through waves. The two most commercially used in a production kitchen are infrared and microwave. Broilers, toasters, and special infrared ovens all transfer heat through heated electric or ceramic elements that reach a high enough temperature to transfer waves of energy at the speed of light through food, to cook it. Microwaves produce invisible waves of energy that cause water molecules in food to rub against each other, creating friction and causing heat that spreads through the food as it cooks. A completely waterless material will not heat in a microwave oven; plates become hot only when heat is conducted to them by the hot food on them.

Cooking changes
The changes that occur during heating make food safe to eat, palatable, tasty, and easier to digest. The effect of cooking also changes the color, texture, aroma, flavor, and nutritional value of food that comes in contact with heat.

The process of cooking affects color in food and sugars react with proteins to cause what is termed "Maillard browning." The longer a food cooks the more color change will take place. If you cook a steak rare it will still retain its red interior, but if you cook it to well done the color will change to a gray interior. Pigments in fruit and vegetables also change with the application of heat. In certain cooking methods vinegar, wine, and lemon juice are sometimes added to help retain the natural color of the product.

All food contains moisture. Cooking removes that moisture the longer the food is cooked. For example, grilling a steak removes the moisture, making the texture firmer. Braising a piece of steak breaks down the connective tissues and coagulates the proteins, making the texture tender and soft. Vegetables will soften as the water in them turns to steam and evaporates. The aroma of the food evolves through the cooking process, making it as pleasing as its taste and flavor. Different cooking methods produce distinctly different flavors. Roasting develops richness, while braising extracts deep flavors from the cooking liquid. Also adding seasoning and flavoring, such as herbs and spices, affects the final flavor of a dish.

The nutritional value of raw food diminishes the longer it is cooked, and different cooking methods either accelerate this process or slow it down. Boiling vegetables, for example, can destroy certain nutrients and some may be lost in the cooking medium. Steaming is a more effective method for retaining as many valuable vitamins as possible.

Cooking times

It takes time for food to cook, to be ready for consumption, and this is affected by three things.
1 Temperature, meaning the temperature of the fat in a deep-fryer, the hot air in a oven, or the surface of the stove top.
2 Speed of heat transfer to the food item. This will depend on the cooking method used. Steaming is a very efficient way to cook. While air is a poor conductor of heat, a blast of steam can burn your hand, but briefly putting your hand in a hot oven will not.
3 Size, temperature of the product, and **characteristics** of the food all determine doneness. A small bread roll cooks faster than a large loaf; a steak straight out of the refrigerator takes longer to cook than a steak at room temperature, while shellfish proteins generally cook faster than red-meat proteins.

Overcooking foods

Cooking usually causes food to undergo favorable changes (for example, flavor and aroma) but the cooking process has to be done properly for the food to retain all the characteristics that are beneficial to us. Overcooking food, by excessive temperature or by cooking the food for too long, destroys the texture, making the product mushy, tough, or stringy. Protein will curdle or toughen, food becomes dry, sugar burns and tastes bitter, green vegetables lose their color and become brown, while valuable nutrients are lost.

15 **Workout: Taste test**

Take two chicken breasts, skin still intact, and season them. Sauté one breast in a sauté pan until the skin is crisp. Turn it over and finish off the cooking in the oven until it is done. You can always refer to a recipe in a cookery book for exact times.

Poach the other chicken breast in chicken stock until it is cooked all the way through. Now taste-test.

You might like one better than the other. Obviously the chicken breast that was sautéed and finished in the oven will be crispy, with a firm texture, while the poached chicken will have an almost jelly-like feel to the skin, but will be very succulent and moist. Two chicken breasts, but different cooking methods, result in two different textures and tastes.

16 **Workout: Research the best**

Research the famous chefs around the world who cook by molecular gastronomy. They are all considered the greatest chefs in the world. Read about how they got into culinary arts, how they design their menus, and the type of food they serve in their world-class restaurants. This will show you how much dedication it took them to reach the top of the culinary ladder and the different styles of cuisine they use.

Food safety

Eating out is one of the best experiences that you, your family, and friends can enjoy. It's the perfect time to relax, have great conversation, celebrate a birthday, conduct a business meeting, and enjoy good food. When we eat out we expect to have a good time, but we also expect to eat well-prepared, safe food in a clean environment, served by pleasant, well-presented staff.

Costs of food-borne illness

- Lawsuits and legal fees
- Negative media exposure
- Loss of customers and sales
- Increase insurance premiums
- Loss of establishment's reputation
- Cost of retaining staff
- Low employee morale
- Employee absenteeism

High-risk groups

These groups of people are considered at high risk because their immune systems may be weak and unable to fight off illness as easily as others at different stages of life:
- The elderly
- Infants and preschool children
- Pregnant women
- People with cancer or HIV/AIDS

The most common symptoms of food-borne illnesses include abdominal cramps, nausea, vomiting, and diarrhea, sometimes followed by high fever. These symptoms may appear within hours, or sometimes days, of the consumption of contaminated foods.

It is important to keep food safe and also to know what affects food safety to prevent good food becoming potentially hazardous. A food-borne illness is transmitted by the food we eat. In general, the hospitality industry does a great job of serving safe food to the public, but food-borne illnesses do occur. These harm people by making them ill and could potentially close the food establishment you work in.

The most important thing to consider is not just the establishment but the victims of food-borne illness; they could experience loss of time at work, medical costs, long-term disability and, possibly, death. You, as an aspiring chef, will play an important role in looking after the food you prepare and serving food that is safe, not only for yourself, family, and friends but also your potential customers. If you know and understand the basics of food safety, then you can help prevent food-related problems.

Forms of contamination

To prevent food-borne illness you need to know what can make food unsafe. There are three main hazards in preparing food: chemical, physical, and biological.

Chemical contaminants are insecticides and cleaning compounds that may accidentally find their way into food.

Physical contaminants can be introduced with careless food handling; these could include bits of broken glass, hairs, or even adhesive dressings (it's important to use colored dressings).

Biological contaminants cause the majority of all food-borne illnesses. These include naturally occurring poisons. The main cause of biological contamination is one of a variety of disease-causing microorganisms known as pathogens. These are responsible for up to 95 percent of all food-borne illnesses.

Food pathogens

Fungi include yeasts and molds and cause food spoilage more often than food-borne illness.

Viral contamination is caused by poor sanitation practices such as not washing the hands after using the bathroom, or by eating shellfish harvested from polluted waters. The best defense against food-borne viruses are good personal hygiene and obtaining shellfish only from certified waters.

Parasites are pathogens that feed and take shelter on other organisms, referred to as "hosts." Amoebas and various worms, such

18 **Workout:** Washing pots

Begin by scraping leftovers into the garbage bin. Then rinse items over the waste disposal. For hand-washing pots, use a three-compartment sink. The water should be at least 110°F (43°C) in the first sink. Then rinse in clear water in the second sink, and sanitize in the third at between 75°F (24°C) and 115°F (46°C). Mechanical dishwashers have to run through the full cycle to clean and properly sanitize equipment.

17 **Workout:** Proper hand-washing

Hand-washing should be done before and after handling raw food, between performing tasks, before putting on single-use gloves, prior to using preparation equipment, and after removing garbage or cleaning work tables. Wet hands and forearms with running water that is a minimum of 100°F (38°C), apply soap to hands, rub hands, arms, and under the fingernails for at least 15 seconds. Rinse off soap under hot water, dry hands with paper towels or a heated air dryer.

19 Workout: Tasting food safely

To become a great chef you must develop great tastebuds, so you must taste everything you make before serving to family, friends, or customers. But never use your fingers when you are tasting food; set up a tasting station. If you are using metal spoons, wash them every time you use them for tasting, or use disposable spoons and throw them away immediately after using. Never reuse or double-dip.

FAT TOM
Remember the six basic conditions for growing and reproducing bacteria:

Food
For pathogens to grow they need a food source, such as protein, from poultry, shellfish, or carbohydrates, for example, potatoes.

Acidity
Pathogens grow best in food that contains little to no acid. Food items with little acid include poultry, beef, milk, and fruit such as cantaloupe.

Temperature
The best temperature for pathogens to grow is 41°F-135°F (5°C-57°C); known as the "danger zone."

Time
If pathogens come into contact with the right food, acidity, and temperature, given time they reach levels high enough to cause illness.

Oxygen
Some pathogens need oxygen, others don't. Those that grow without oxygen will flourish in cooked rice.

Moisture
Fruits and vegetables, which are moist, are ideal breeding grounds for pathogens, along with raw meats and shellfish.

as *Trichinella spirali*, which can be found in under-cooked pork, are among the parasites that contaminate food products. Bacteria are responsible for most food-borne illnesses. Bacteria require six basic conditions for growing and reproduction: food, acidity, temperature, time, oxygen (some), and moisture. To help remember these conditions, remember the acronym "FAT TOM" (see also box right). Give bacteria FAT TOM and they can reproduce every 20 minutes, into large enough numbers to cause food poisoning. Many foods offer the right conditions to be called potentially hazardous foods. These include meats, poultry, seafood, tofu, and dairy products, also some vegetables, grains, cooked rice, beans, and pastas.

Cross-contamination happens when disease-causing bacteria are transferred from one contaminated surface to another. Excellent personal hygiene and good working practices are the best defense against cross-contamination.

Time and temperature control
Once pathogens have established in a food source they will either thrive or be destroyed, depending on how long they are allowed to stay in the so-called danger zone of 41°F-135°F (5°C-57°C). Most pathogens will be destroyed or will not reproduce at temperatures above 135°F (57°C). Storing at temperatures below 41°F (5°C) will slow down the cycle of reproduction. Foods left in the danger zone for periods longer than four hours could cause food poisoning.

Refrigeration and freezer units should be regularly cleaned and the food rotated as it is being used. Refrigerators should be kept between 36°F-40°F (2°C-4°C). Raw products must be stored below, and away from, cooked foods, to prevent cross-contamination. Keep dry food areas clean, dry, and well ventilated, and store goods off the ground.

Personal hygiene
Good personal hygiene can prevent most food-borne illnesses. This means that you must shower before work and keep your hair clean at all times. Wear a hat and tie long hair back, making sure it is covered. Wear clean clothing every day, remove aprons when taking out the

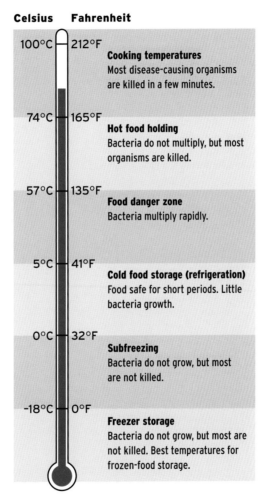

Celsius	Fahrenheit	
100°C	212°F	**Cooking temperatures** Most disease-causing organisms are killed in a few minutes.
74°C	165°F	**Hot food holding** Bacteria do not multiply, but most organisms are killed.
57°C	135°F	**Food danger zone** Bacteria multiply rapidly.
5°C	41°F	**Cold food storage (refrigeration)** Food safe for short periods. Little bacteria growth.
0°C	32°F	**Subfreezing** Bacteria do not grow, but most are not killed.
-18°C	0°F	**Freezer storage** Bacteria do not grow, but most are not killed. Best temperatures for frozen-food storage.

garbage or using the bathroom. Change aprons when they are dirty. Remove jewelry from hands and arms. You should wash your hands frequently, especially after using the bathroom. Use gloves, tongs, and deli tissue when you are handling ready-to-serve food.

Your workstation
It is essential to keep all work areas, including tables, walls, storage areas, and garbage containers, scrupulously clean. Equipment or surfaces, such as knives, preparation tables, and cutting boards, that come into contact with food must be cleaned and sanitized before and after use.

Knives—the essential tools

Just as an artist needs paint and brushes and a photographer needs a camera, for you to become a professional chef you need to select some good-quality tools, in this case knives. The set of knives you choose will become as important to you as your own fingers—every knife becoming an extension of your own hand as you work.

Your basic kit

To start your knife kit, buy only the basic knives that you need to use every day. As you continue to work, whether in the professional kitchen or at college, your knife kit will grow, to include special knives that are intended for specific jobs.

1 Chef's knife

This is an all-purpose knife that can be used to chop, slice, and mince. The blade is normally 8–12 in (20–30 cm) in length.

2 Paring knife

Much shorter than the chef's knife, the paring knife ranges from 2–4 in (5–10 cm) in length and is used for preparing vegetables and fruits.

3 Boning knife

With a very rigid blade, usually about 6 in (15 cm) in length and thinner than the chef's knife, this knife is used for separating the meat from the bone of a carcass.

4 Filleting knife

A very flexible, thin blade used for filleting fish, this knife is about the same length as the boning knife.

5 Palette knife

With a flexible blade, this knife is used to spread fillings and glazes rather than slicing and cutting.

6 and 7 Heavy- and fine-grained steels

These tools are used to keep the edge of your knife sharp and in alignment after you have sharpened it on the stone (see Workouts 21 and 22).

8 Vegetable peeler

This tool is used to peel the skin from various vegetables and fruits.

The knife's main parts

There are three main parts to the knife blade, which can be used for different tasks. These are: the tip, the center, and the heel. The tip is where the knife is thinnest and narrowest—use this part on small items or on delicate work. The center of the blade is used for most of the general work, while the heel, the thickest and heaviest part of the knife, is for chopping or coarse work.

20 Workout: Learn your knife anatomy

Familiarize yourself with the different parts of the knife and the features that you should look for when you are shopping for a good-quality knife.

Tang
This is a continuation of the blade, extending into the knife's handle.

Blade
A blade made from high-carbon steel will keep its edge longer than other types. Make sure the blade is "taper-ground"—forged from a single sheet of metal.

Rivets
These hold the tang and handle together and should be smooth and flush with the surface.

Handle
Rosewood is the best handle material because it is hard and resistant, however many handles are hard wood infused with plastic, riveted to the tang (as shown here).

Bolster
A feature of a good-quality knife, the bolster helps to balance the knife and prevents your hand from slipping down the blade.

21 Workout: Using a stone

Lubricate the coarsest side of the stone with water or mineral oil. Always sharpen the knife edge in the same direction.

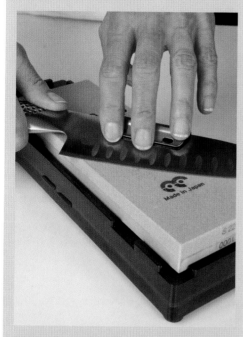

Hold the knife at a 20-degree angle and run the entire edge of the knife over the surface of the stone. Make ten strokes of equal pressure on each side of the blade. Then turn the stone over and water or oil the other surface. Repeat the same actions as before, then wash and dry the knife before using your steel.

22 Workout: Using a steel

Use the steel immediately after using a stone, and also between sharpenings, to keep the knife edge sharp and in alignment. Keep the knife at an angle to the steel and maintain even pressure. Repeat the strokes on the opposite side of the knife to straighten the edge properly.

1 Hold the steel with your thumb and fingers behind the safety guard. Place the heel at the bottom of the steel.

2 With the knife at a 20-degree angle to the steel, and keeping pressure even, draw the knife along the steel so that the entire edge touches the steel.

3 Continue until you reach the tip of the knife. Repeat on the other side of the knife. Five strokes on each side will do the trick.

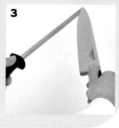

WARNING—take your time, speed will come with practice.

23 Workout: Practice the basic cutting holds

Whether you are left- or right-handed, one hand controls the knife while the other (your guiding hand) controls what you are cutting.

Holding the knife
Grasp the handle of the knife, but keep your thumb and forefinger on the blade. This might feel strange to begin with, but it gives you great control over the blade. Hold the knife with one hand. Your other hand (your guiding hand) holds whatever you are cutting.

Your guiding hand
Hold the item to be cut firmly and curl your fingertips under, out of the way of the blade, making sure that the knife slides down your knuckles and not your fingertips. The position of your fingers is very important since it controls the cut and keeps your fingertips safe.

1 Try forming your hand into a claw shape before you start. Get comfortable with this before picking up your knife.

2 Hold the item to be cut in the same claw shape. Arrange your hand so that your knife just brushes the knuckles.

Key pointers

A good-quality knife will last a lifetime if you look after it properly, so respect your knives and keep them sharp. A good, sharp knife not only performs better, but is safer to use because you use less force when you are cutting.

• Keep your knives clean—not just the blade but the whole knife, from tip to handle. Always use a chopping board because this will prevent the blade from dulling.
• It is vital to carry your knife held straight down at your side, with the sharp edge facing behind you, and let people around you know that you are carrying it.
• Lay the knife down flat on your chopping board if you are not using it and do not let it extend past its edge.
• If you knock your knife off the chopping board, **NEVER** attempt to catch it.
• Keep your knives properly stored. A good way of doing this is in a knife roll, with your name on it, but remember to keep this clean too.
• It is wise to engrave your name on your knives, especially if you have gone to the trouble of selecting a good-quality set that may have cost a considerable sum.

Hand tools

To be successful in any kitchen you need a good understanding of all the necessary equipment that you will be using on a day-to-day basis. Most hand tools are made from stainless steel, aluminum, or plastic.

Pots and pans

• A rondeau (rahn-DOH) is a wide pan with 6-8 in (15-20 cm) sides. Good for braises and stews, it is used to cook big roasts or large quantities.
• A stockpot is a large, tall-sided pot used mainly for making stocks or soup.
• A saucepot is a versatile pan similar to a stockpot, only smaller, with straight sides.
• A saucepan is smaller than a saucepot and can have either straight or flared sides with one handle.
• A double boiler is a set of pans that fit one on top of the other. The lower pan is filled with water, which is then heated to cook foods that require a gentle heat without direct contact with heat.
• A sauteuse (saw-TOOZ) is a sauté pan with sloped or rounded sides, which makes it easy to toss ingredients.
• A sautoir (saw-TWAHR) is a sauté pan with straight sides and is used for pan-frying.
• A wok is mainly used for stir-frying. Bowl-shaped and often made out of black steel, it must be brushed with oil and stored dry.
• A cast-iron skillet is a frying pan made to withstand high temperatures.
• A roasting pan is a large, rectangular metal pan with 2-5 in (5-12 cm) sides, used for roasting or baking.

Just like your set of knives (see pages 22-23) you need to choose hand tools wisely and buy quality to last a lifetime. In a professional kitchen you will find a wide variety of cookware; choosing the right pot or pan may be critical to the success of the dish. A pot is taller than it is wide, whereas a pan is wider than it is tall. The best materials to cook with are good conductors of heat; the most commonly used are copper, stainless steel, and aluminum. Whatever material you choose, look for well-made, thick, heavy-based pans with strong rivets or welds attaching the handles. Thinner metals will give uneven heating and buckle and warp over time.

Copper

Copper has long been used in the top kitchens because it is an excellent conductor of heat, cooking food evenly. The only drawback is that it is very expensive and needs to be cleaned often. Also copper can react to certain foods, which is why pans are lined with stainless steel.

Stainless steel

Stainless-steel cookware is less expensive than copper and lighter to lift, but it is a poor conductor of heat and creates a cooking surface with hotspots that can burn sauces and cook unevenly. The best stainless-steel cookware to buy has copper or nickel bases for better conduction.

Aluminum

Aluminum is a good conductor of heat, costs less than copper and stainless steel and is the most widely used material in commercial kitchens.

Other kitchen tools

Bowls come in many sizes and are used for mixing and storing product. They are usually made of stainless steel.

Measuring cups and spoons come in different sizes and are great tools to use in a commercial kitchen and also at home. Following recipes requires ingredients to be measured accurately and measuring cups and spoons are essential.

Scales come in a variety of types; the balance beam scale is well favored by bakers to weigh out flour for bread and pastries. Portion scales are a small set of scales, ideal for weighing small or individual ingredients. They are available as mechanical spring-type scales or electronic scales with a digital readout.

Thermometers come in several types. They are an essential kitchen tool for ensuring safe food-handling practices and are used during cooking, holding, and cooling. You need to have an "instant read" thermometer, which registers temperature within a few seconds of being used. It is the ideal tool for making sure cooked items reach a desired doneness and correct internal temperature. The temperature range is 0°F-220°F (-17°C-104°C). Thermocouple thermometers are electronic devices that measure and record temperatures very accurately. Laser thermometers use a laser beam to measure the temperature of the food without actually touching it. Their drawback is that they only measure the surface temperature, not internally.

A mandoline is a kitchen tool that slices food by pushing it against a very sharp blade; it can make thick or thin slices, to stick cuts, to julienne.

24 Workout: Experimenting with a mandoline

A mandoline is a manually operated slicer made of stainless steel or hardened plastic with adjustable slicing blades. It can be used to make julienne and waffle-cut slices. Pass the food along the blade to achieve even slices. Make sure you use the hand guard or a steel glove.

1 Cut the vegetable into a manageable size that fits into your hand.

2 Position the vegetable under the guard and, using even strokes, run the vegetable up and down the blade of the mandoline.

25 Workout: Using a bamboo matt to make sushi

The cuisine of Japan is dominated by rice and fish; these two staples combined making sushi (*szu-she*). Sushi originated as a way of preserving fish on the fishing boats by salting the fish and then packing it in vinegared rice. Originally the fish was eaten and the rice discarded. You will need sushi rice, fillings, *nori* (seaweed paper), and a *sudare* (bamboo mat).

1 Place the nori on the sudare, wet your hands with cold water and spread the sushi rice over the lower two-thirds.

2 Lay the strips of the filling across the middle of the rice.

3 Holding the filling in place, lift the corner of the mat and roll up. Wet your finger and run it along the nori to seal.

4 Wet your knife and slice through the sushi, cleaning and wetting your knife between each cut. Aim for six to eight pieces.

26 Workout: Making a paper lid

Using a paper lid is a great way to evenly cook vegetables, rice dishes, braises, and delicate fish dishes. It is easy to make and every kitchen has a supply of parchment paper. When you have made the lid, brush it with melted butter or lightly rub it with butter or olive oil.

1 Fold a piece of parchment paper into a cone shape by making four folds inward.
2 Using a pair of kitchen scissors, cut off a small piece of the tip of the cone.
3 Cut the cone shape to the size of the pan.
4 Open up the cone and you should have a circle large enough to cover the top of the pan, with a small hole to let the steam out.

Straining equipment
Strainers come in all different shapes and sizes, for various kitchen purposes.
• A china cap is a cone-shaped strainer used to remove lumps from sauces.
• A colander is a large bowl-shaped strainer used to drain large amounts of product, such as cooked vegetables, or for draining salad leaves after being washed.
• A chinois (*SHEEN wah*) is a type of china cap, but with a very fine mesh, which is good for straining small particles from sauces.
• A ricer is a cylindrical metal sieve with an attached plunger. It's used for pushing cooked foods through small holes into rice-shaped pieces; ideal for mashed potatoes.
• A drum sieve is a circular-shaped sieve for sifting large quantities of dry ingredients or straining puréed foods.

27 Workout: Using a ricer

A ricer/food mill is used to purée and strain food at the same time. A hand-crank turns the blade, pushing the food through a perforated disk. Most ricers/food mills have different-sized disks with various-sized holes. Make sure you choose one that comes apart easily, so that it is easy to clean. Place the food into the hopper and position the ricer/mill over a clean bowl, turn the handle, and the puréed product will fall through into the bowl.

Electric tools

In today's modern kitchen a vast array of specialized electrical equipment is available to make the chef's life easier. The challenge is to select the right appliance for the job.

Power equipment safety rules

1 Never operate a piece of equipment until you have been trained in its use. You must be supervised the first time you operate it. You also need to be trained in how to break down the equipment parts to clean them and how to put them back together in perfect working order.

2 Safety switches are designed for your safety and for the safe operation of the machine. If a piece of equipment requires a safety guard to be in place while using, NEVER use that equipment without the guard being in place. NEVER bypass hand guards.

3 ALWAYS disconnect power tools or equipment when not in use. And always disconnect power tools and equipment before cleaning or disassembling.

4 If the machine is not working, never try to fix it yourself. Report the problem to your supervisor immediately. Make sure you have disconnected the machine from the power supply and leave a notice on the equipment stating what the problem is.

From grinding, slicing, mixing, and puréeing to making fresh pasta, hot beverages, and donut glazes, technology brings new tools to simplify the cooking process. In this section we discuss the basic electrical tools you will use every day in a commercial kitchen, and possibly at home too.

Many jobs that a chef would have done in the past can now be done quickly and efficiently by modern equipment. But this is equipment that can burn, cut, smash, mangle, and amputate parts of your body. This is not meant to frighten. Rather it is to instill a healthy respect for operating procedures and safety requirements. Machines are intended to be labor-saving, but this usually requires using them to process large amounts of food at once. If you have only a small number of carrots to slice, for example, it is more efficient to hand-slice them than set up the slicing attachment, pass the carrots through, break the machine down, and clean it, not to mention put it together again. This is why it is important to develop excellent manual skills.

Food processors

Food processors make grinding, puréeing, and blending easy for the chef. Attachments can be added for slicing, shredding, and dicing. Processors come in different sizes and different strengths for tasks large and small. Food processors fit easily onto tabletops and so into kitchens of all sizes.

Slicing foods evenly
A food slicer is a very valuable machine that slices foods more evenly and uniformly than can be achieved by hand. This is helpful for portion control and for reducing the amount of waste.

Blenders

Blenders mix, purée, and liquefy foods by using high-velocity blades, and come in two basic designs for the commercial kitchen. The liquidizer/bar blender has a motorized base and a covered jug, or container, which sits on it. The blades are located at the bottom of the jug, into which food is dropped, and this is covered with a lid. When the machine is turned on the food cannot splash out. An immersion blender, stick blender, or hand blender can be a one-piece or two-piece machine, depending on the size of the blender. Usually the handle holds the motor, while the shaft holds the blades at the other end. The shaft and blades are immersed in a container of liquid, such as a pot of soup, and the food is puréed in the same container that it was prepared in. Both blenders are very easy to clean and store.

Mixers

Mixers come in tabletop models, which hold 5-20 quarts (5-20 liters) and floor models, which hold up to 140 quarts (133 liters). Adaptor rings enable several bowl sizes to be used on one machine. Mixers are used to knead bread doughs, whip cream or mayonnaise, and mix pastries.

Slicing machines

It is very important to be trained in using a slicer before using it. A slicer uses a rotating blade to slice foods evenly, thickly or thinly. A carriage holds the food in place, allowing your hands to remain well out of the way while the

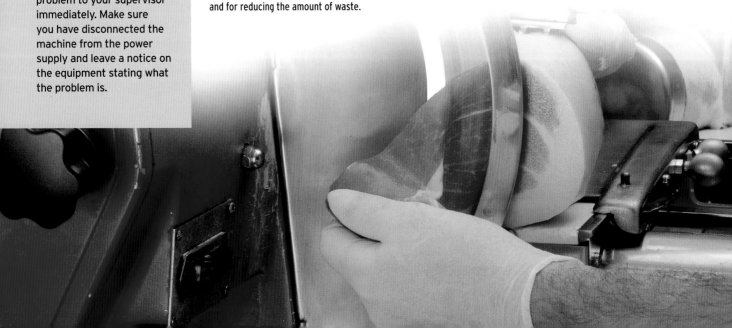

machine is running. Slicing machines can easily cause injuries, so be very careful when using, assembling, or cleaning.

Meat grinders

A meat grinder is either a free-standing machine or an attachment that can be used on a buffalo chopper or food-mixing machine. It grinds meat, fish, or other food products into coarse or fine textures, which can be used to make pâtés, sausages, and terrines. An auger, or worm, forces the food through a feeding tube, past a rotating blade, and through the holes of the die. Dies come in different sizes for different textures. Always use a plastic plunger to push the food through the feed tube. Never use your hands.

Buffalo chopper

A buffalo chopper is a machine that chops large quantities of food. The machine has a rotating

bowl into which the food is placed. Once switched on, the bowl revolves around a set of rotating blades that chop the food into small pieces.

Deep-fryers

Deep fryers have one purpose: to cook foods in very hot fat. They come in three models: standard, which is powered by gas or electricity; automatic, which automatically removes food from the fat after a preset time has elapsed, and pressure fryers, which cook foods very rapidly, covered under pressure, even at low temperatures.

Microwave ovens

Microwave ovens have special tubes in them that generate microwave radiation, which creates heat inside food. Microwave cooking is discussed in more detail in the section on food science (see page 18).

Floor mixers
These are ideal for helping the chef or baker mix or whip large batches of food.

---

28 **Workout:** Mixing ingredients

You will find that a tabletop, or vertical, mixer will be an indispensible tool in your kitchen, whether commercial or at home. Experiment with the three common mixing attachments: the whip/whisk (used for whipping egg whites, creams, and mousses), the paddle (used for general mixing), and the dough hook (used for kneading breads).

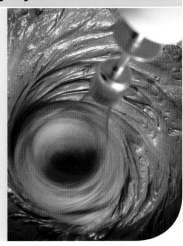

---

29 **Workout:** Know your equipment

There are many different manufacturers of the same types of equipment, so it's important to familiarize yourself with them. For example, all food processors grind, purée, and blend food using the same operating principles. Each model is slightly different, if only in the location of the switches. You might have two or three food processers in a commercial kitchen. It is important to know how each one operates and what attachments can be used with it.

---

30 **Workout:** Using a deep-fryer

Tempura, or the techniques of dipping fish and vegetables into a light batter and deep-frying, comes from the word "tempora," a Latin word meaning "times," which was used by Spanish and Portuguese missionaries. This refers to Christian holy days when meat was forbidden and Christians were only allowed to eat fish and vegetables.

Recipe
- 1 egg
- 1 cup (250 ml) sparkling water
- 1 cup (140 g) flour
- ½ tsp salt
- Mixed vegetables, such as mushroom, broccoli florets, and zucchini, or shrimp and small cuts of fish

Beat the eggs in a large stainless-steel bowl and add the very cold sparkling water. Add the flour and incorporate it, leaving some lumps in the batter from the flour (overmixing develops gluten, which is undesirable). Wash and trim the vegetables into even sizes. You may need to blanche the broccoli. Dip the vegetables or shrimp/fish into the batter and drop them one at a time into the deep-fryer. Cook until it is done and serve with a dipping sauce.

Getting started
Stoves & kitchen equipment

Stoves are the most important piece of equipment in any kitchen. Without heat you cannot prepare, cook, and finish the many different dishes served in a restaurant or at home.

Most ranges and ovens are powered by gas or electricity. The stove top is known as the "range" and types of ranges commonly found in commercial kitchens are open-burners, griddles, flat-tops, and induction tops. The oven is usually located below the range and is either a conventional oven, a convection oven, or a combination oven.

Gone are the days when chefs would walk into the kitchen in the morning, turn on all the ranges and keep them on all day. The cost of energy today has made this practice obsolete in almost every kitchen, but fortunately modern equipment takes less time to heat. Chefs now plan their production so that equipment requiring a lot of energy is not kept on for long periods when it is not in use. You, as an aspiring chef, need to know the preheating times of all the cooking equipment in your kitchen, so that you can avoid turning equipment on until you need to.

Open-burner range
Burners can be either electric coils or gas flames. Quick to heat, you should turn them off right after use. Limited to one pot or pan per burner, open-burner ranges usually have six burners.

Flat-top
Flat-top burners cover the whole top of the range with a heavy cast-iron plate, meaning that more space is available for cookware. The middle of the range is the hottest spot, with the outside being cooler. A thick flat-top requires preheating.

Induction cooktop
Induction cooktops are slowly making their way into commercial kitchens. The top itself does not become hot; it works by magnetically agitating the molecules in the steel, nickel, iron, and alloys in the pots and pans. This means that there are no hot surfaces or open flames and no preheating, so you use less energy. The drawbacks are that the equipment is very expensive, and you need to use special cookware.

Ovens
Conventional ovens are the most familiar part of any range unit; the oven operates simply by heating air in an enclosed box. Preheating is required and you must make sure that the pilot light is on before turning on the gas.

Convection ovens contain fans that circulate hot air rapidly throughout the oven. Foods cook more quickly and evenly and at lower temperatures than in a conventional oven. When cooking, check the recommended temperature and reduce it by typically 25°F-50°F (14°C-28°C) lower than a conventional oven. Watch cooking times carefully.

Combination ovens use a combination of convection heat and steam to cook food. This oven is also known as a "combi" or "combo" oven. The moisture of the steam greatly reduces cooking time. This type of oven can operate as a convection oven, in combination mode, or as a convection steamer.

Working the line
This is the term used when you are cooking food on the range; it is usually very fast-paced, so building skills is essential to success.

31 Workout: Flame heights

Try to control the water temperature for the following moist-heat cooking methods: boiling means to cook in a liquid that is bubbling rapidly at 212°F (100°C). If you turn down the heat to 185°F-205°F (85°C-96°C), you will be simmering. Now lower the temperature again to 160°F-180°F (71°C-82°C) and you are at poaching temperature. Notice the difference. Boiling is usually reserved for vegetables and starches, while simmering and poaching are used for more delicate foods such as fish or eggs.

32 Workout: Oven-roasted tomatoes

These tomatoes are remarkably easy to make and very tasty. Remove the core and cut the tomatoes into halves. Arrange them on a sheet pan. Mix olive oil and chopped garlic, shallots, basil, oregano, and thyme and drizzle over the tomatoes. Season with salt and pepper, roast in the oven at 275°F (135°C) for one to two hours. They are ideal in salads, pasta dishes, or served on toasted bread.

A **cook-hold oven** is designed to cook food at lower temperatures, 180°F–225°F (82°C–107°C). This type of oven is very good for roasting large roasts of meat such as a forerib of beef or a turkey, since the lower temperatures mean less shrinkage. The oven can be programed so that after cooking has been completed the oven switches to "holding" mode, which keeps the food at the correct temperature until needed.

Microwave ovens work by bombarding food with microwave radiation, which causes the water molecules in the food to vibrate and create heat, which cooks the food. Due to limited capacity, microwaves are primarily used for reheating and thawing individual portions.

Steaming

Steamers use water heated to the point of vaporizing to apply heat to food. This is a moist method of cooking, which is ideal for steaming vegetables, stews, and braises but which is not good for crisp pastries or breads.

Convection steamers cook food in perforated hotel pans placed into the steamer. The food product is then cooked by a circulation of steam.

Pressure steamers are very similar to convection steamers, though a pressure steamer's chamber is tightly sealed, allowing pressure to build, holding more heat energy, and cooking food more rapidly. The steamer needs

33 Workout: Practicing baking

Baking is very similar to roasting and it's important that you experiment with the technique as much as possible; the subtle difference between them is often when describing the food on the menu. An example might be oven-roasted chicken (cooked in the oven uncovered) while lasagne would be described as baked (with moisture and a sauce). Freshly made oven-baked bread rolls are a hit at home and in any restaurant.

to be depressurized before you open the door. This type of steamer is ideal for high-volume institutions.

Broilers, salamanders, and grills use radiant heat for cooking. Broilers use a radiant source above the food, which browns and cooks it. A smaller, less powerful, broiler, used for browning food rather than cooking it fully, is called a "salamander." The name is believed to be associated with the browned food changing color, just like a salamander changing skin color. When a radiant heat source is located below the food product, this is called a "grill" or "char-grill," which can use an electric element to radiate heat or a gas flame, or use charcoal to give a smoky flavor to the finished food.

A commercial kitchen
Stepping into a commercial kitchen for the first time can be intimidating, due to the array of cooking apparatus, the number of different pots and pans, and the kitchen layout. This is why it is important to know the equipment, operating procedures, safety features, and temperature settings to avoid injuries and ensure properly cooked, safe food.

Stocks, soups, & sauces

Making a great stock is considered to be one of the greatest tests of a chef's craft. A stock is the foundation of soups, sauces, and most braises and stews. It is a very basic chef's skill that you need to perfect by making it over and over again, by learning what elements are used, and how to develop flavor and richness.

Soups are becoming ever more popular with customers today, perhaps due to the increase in nutrition-consciousness or just a desire to eat lighter meals full of flavor that can easily satisfy the heartiest of appetites.

Sauces are believed by many chefs to be the finishing touches for many dishes; very often when you eat out it is the sauce served with the meat or the fish that you remember most. A well-created sauce will not dominate or hide the food but enhance, season, and complement it. In this section you will learn the basic sauces and what thickens them, a roux, a starch, or a purée, all fundamentals you need to know in order to become an accomplished chef. You will learn why stocks, soups, and sauces are so important in your repertoire and why basic techniques of making them are the building blocks for creating a wide variety of appetizing dishes.

32 | Spices

Spices are aromatics that are produced from berries, fruits, bark, seeds, and the roots of plants. They are used in cooking to bring flavor to savory or sweet dishes, but without the addition of extra fat or calories. Spices come from all over the world; they can be bought fresh but are usually sold in dried form.

While the spices are whole or dried, they should keep their flavor for at least six to nine months, if you store them correctly. You should keep them in containers with airtight lids and placed out of direct sunlight, in a cool place. Once you have ground the spices, aim to use them as quickly as possible, since they lose their flavors rapidly. It's a good idea to add dried spices early in the cooking process so that their flavors develop while the dish is cooking. In some dishes, such as Indian curries, you cook spices first to release their aromas and then grind them before you add them to the dish.

Using spices successfuly to create complex flavors comes with practice and patience. One of the first things you, as an aspiring chef, should learn is the timeless combinations of flavorings that you can achieve with the help of spices, such as spinach with nutmeg or caraway seeds with rye bread. Learn the basics first, but don't be afraid to experiment with new combinations. However, always bear in mind the following guidelines:

Spice guidelines

• Never overpower the primary ingredient with a spice in order to disguise its taste or aroma.
• Balance the spices you are using so as not to overwhelm the palate.
• Don't use spices to disguise poor product—such as poor-quality meat.
• Use spices sparingly and taste and season food frequently while it is cooking.

34 Workout: Toasting spices

To release the flavor of your spices, take a nonstick frying pan and gently warm it over medium heat. Add the whole spices and shake or stir them until they are fragrant. Be careful not to burn them, because they scorch very easily. Transfer them to a paper towel and allow them to cool before you grind them.

Commonly used spices

Spice	Form	Usage
Allspice (1)	whole/ground	relish, braised meats
Anise (2)	whole/ground	Asian cuisine, breads
Cardamom (3)	ground	rice, sweet dough, curries
Chilies (4)	chopped/powdered	meat and vegetable dishes
Cinnamon (5)	whole/ground	compotes, fruit pies
Galangal (6)	chopped/powdered	Asian cuisine, especially soups
Mace (7)	ground	sausage, pâté, bread
Peppercorns (8)	ground	meat and vegetable dishes
Saffron (9)	threads/ground	rice, breads, soups
Tamarind (10)	dried/fresh chopped	pickles, chutneys, sauces, drinks
Wasabi (11)	grated	sauces, snacks

35 Workout: Grinding spices

Use a pestle and mortar to grind the spices once they have cooled after toasting. If you are dealing with large amounts you could use a small electric coffee grinder, but remember to reserve it for spices and don't use it for grinding coffee. If you do not have a pestle and mortar or a coffee grinder, put the spices into a zip-lock bag, place a tea towel over it, and crush the spices with a rolling pin or heavy saucepan.

36 Workout: Preparing fresh chili

There are many varieties of chili peppers, both hot and sweet, and they range in color, flavor, and heat. Most of their heat is contained in the seeds and veins. ALWAYS remember to wear gloves or wash your hands thoroughly after preparing chilis since the oil in them will burn your eyes and other sensitive areas of your body if you touch them with contaminated hands.

1 Using your paring knife, cut the chili in half lengthwise. Scrape out the seeds and remove the white veins from the sides.

2 Cut the chili into fine strips, then slice or chop into small dice.

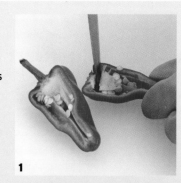
1

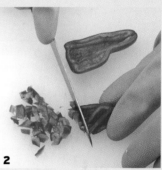
2

37 Workout: Preparing fresh ginger

Fresh ginger is known as a "hand" because it looks rather like a group of knobbly fingers. Most recipes will ask for a measurement of ginger such as a 1-sq-in (2.5-cm) piece. The hand is covered in a thin skin, which you normally remove before use. Practice peeling and chopping ginger in various ways.

Peeling with a paring knife
Take the ginger in one hand and hold your paring knife in the other. Peel just under the skin, letting your knife glide over the lumps and bumps easily.

Peeling with a spoon
Hold the ginger between thumb and index finger, take a metal spoon and rest your thumb against the ginger. Scrape downward—the skin should come off. Repeat, rotating the piece until you have removed all the skin.

Blocking off
Place the piece of ginger on the chopping board and, using your chef's knife, cut off the curved edges until you have made a rectangular shape, which you can then slice into rounds, strips, or dice.

Julienne
1 Holding the ginger with the claw grip, slice lengthwise into thin slabs.

2 Pile the slabs together and slice very thinly into julienne strips.

Rounds
Holding the ginger with the claw grip, slice into rounds.

Dice
Using the claw grip rotate the julienne through 90 degrees and finely chop the ginger into dice.

34 | Herbs

Herbs are available in a variety of forms and flavors and are used to accentuate the flavor of food. They are derived from a large variety of plants and their leaves, stems, buds, or flowers can be used whole, ground, or chopped to add flavor to all kinds of dishes. Aroma is a very good indicator of quality in both fresh and dried herbs.

Herbs add neither fat nor sodium and virtually no calories to dishes. Dried herbs are widely used because they are readily available. If you are using dried herbs, use a smaller quantity since the flavor is more concentrated than when they are fresh. For example, if your recipe asks for 1 oz (1 tbs) fresh chives, use only ½ oz (½ tbs) dried. Most dried herbs are added to dishes at the beginning of cooking as they need time to develop their distinct flavor, while it is best to add most fresh herbs at the end of cooking. But if you are using fresh herbs in uncooked preparations, such as salsa or salads, then you should add them well in advance of serving to bring out their best qualities.

Keep dried herbs in airtight containers and stored in a cool, dry place, out of direct sunlight, since the light will destroy the delicate flavors. If they are stored properly, dried herbs should

last for between two and three months. When purchasing fresh herbs, look for an even color from tip to root, healthy-looking leaves and stems, and no wilting, brown spots, or pest damage. Store fresh herbs loosely wrapped in a damp paper towel. Place in plastic bags to retain moisture and reduce wilting, label, and refrigerate at 34°F–40°F (2°C–4°C).

Commonly used herbs

Herb	Uses
Basil (1)	salads, tomatoes, egg dishes, fish dishes, lamb, pizza, breads
Bay (2)	soups, stews, meat, seafood, vegetables
Chervil (3)	soups, salads, fish dishes, vegetables
Chives (4)	eggs, fish, soups, chicken, potatoes
Cilantro (5)	salsa, salads, shellfish, Mexican cuisine
Dill (6)	soups, pickles
Marjoram (7)	meats, sauces
Mint (8)	sauces, soups, desserts
Oregano (9)	sauces, meats, vegetables, pizzas
Parsley (10)	garnish, potato dishes, rice dishes, meats, soups
Rosemary (11)	meats, Mediterranean dishes
Tarragon (12)	French cuisine, chicken, fish dishes, egg dishes
Thyme (13)	pork dishes, stews, soups, tomatoes

38 Workout: Washing herbs

Washing ensures that the herbs are completely free of impurities. These include such things as soil, dirt, sand, or insects, and it is very important that any insecticides used during growing are thoroughly removed. Before you start washing, check the herbs for freshness and remove and discard any rotten or wilted leaves or stems.

1 Fill a large basin or sink with enough fresh, cold water to completely cover the herbs.

2 Using your hands, submerge the herbs in the water and shake them. Then lift out the herbs and pour away the water.

3 Repeat the washing process until the water is clear. Shake excess water from the herbs and pat dry. Use straight away or store for later use.

Grow your own herbs

Sometimes you'll find you don't have access to fresh herbs right when you need them. You may be cooking and suddenly decide you need parsley, but have none to hand. One of the easiest ways to solve this problem is to grow your own. Herbs are one of the easiest things you will ever grow and they are the perfect plant to have indoors, such as on a kitchen windowsill.

Many professional chefs prefer to grow their herbs in their kitchen, where they can access them easily during cooking, knowing that they are completely fresh. You can buy herbs as seedlings or you can start your plants from seeds. Whatever you decide, give it a try and see how easy it is.

39 Workout: Chopping chives

First, remove the elastic band holding the chives, if there is one, then wash the chives and dry with a paper towel. Place them on your cutting board and take out your chef's knife.

Holding the chives with one hand, cut through them with your knife, using a rolling motion. The knife should roll from the tip to the heel without leaving the cutting board. Take your time and cut finely and evenly.

40 Workout: Chopping rosemary

Make sure you thoroughly wash the rosemary stalks (as shown in Workout 38) and dry them thoroughly before you start processing them. Rosemary is one of the more robust herbs, with a strong flavor. Use it to enhance your stocks and stews.

1 Holding the stalk of the rosemary in one hand, gently pull the leaves back on themselves with your other hand. The leaves should come away from the stalk very easily.

2 Continue until you have removed all the leaves from the stalks. Pile the leaves together.

3 Grip the rosemary using the claw method, so that your fingertips are out of the way while you are chopping. Use a smooth movement, rolling the knife from tip to heel, to get a very fine cut.

36 | Stocks

Stock, or "fond," as the French call it, is a true cooking fundamental. It forms the base of great soups, sauces, stews, and braised dishes.

Stock is made from a combination of bones, vegetables, seasonings, and liquids and is the very essence of cooking. To become a great chef you need to know how to produce a great stock, with plenty of body, flavor, clarity, and color. It is false economy to neglect this very critical part of the culinary art.

The most important aspect of any stock is its flavor, and a strong, pure stock is best achieved using quality ingredients, paying attention to the ratio of solids to liquid, and the length of the cooking process.

Five basic stocks

There are five basic stocks that are generally used by all chefs all around the world: white, brown, fish, vegetable, and court bouillon.

White stock is made with chicken, veal, or beef bones, vegetables, and water, and it remains relatively colorless during the cooking process. Brown stock is made with chicken, veal, beef, or game bones, and vegetables that have been browned in the oven. It is then simmered in water to produce a rich-flavored, dark-colored stock.

Fish stock is made by cooking fish bones or crustacean shells with vegetables in simmering

A flavorful base
A good stock is a flavorful liquid produced from simmering bones, vegetables, herbs, and spices with a cooking liquid to extract a concentrated flavor that can be used as a base for soups and sauces.

Essential parts of a stock

For good flavor and body, use meaty bones and fish bones. Bones from younger animals give the best-quality stock. Make sure you rinse the bones before putting them into the stockpot. Trim and cut mirepoix to a size required for the stock. Onions, leeks, and celery are the main vegetables to use, then your bouquet garni containing the aromatics, and finally the water.

Water
Vegetables
Bones
Flavorings

water for just a short time, to produce a strong-flavored, relatively colorless, liquid. Vegetable stock is made of a mixture of vegetables, seasoning, and water, while court bouillon is made by simmering vegetables and seasoning in water with wine or vinegar. This is normally used to poach fish or vegetables.

Basic ingredients

The basic ingredients for any good-quality stock are: bones, mirepoix (a mixture of onions, carrots, and celery, which is added to the stock to enhance the flavor and aroma), seasoning, and liquid. The denser the bone is, the longer it takes to cook into a well-flavored stock. Veal or beef bones usually take between six and eight hours of gentle simmering, while chicken bones take between three and four hours to produce a good-quality stock. Chicken stock is the most used stock. The best bones for beef and veal come from younger animals, which have a high percentage of collagen, giving richness

41 Workout: Preparing chicken stock

To make a clear stock, rinse the chicken bones with cold water to remove impurities, then blanch in boiling water to clean them before starting.

Recipe
- 15 lb (6.8 kg) chicken bones (neck and back)
- 3 gal (11.5 liters) cold water
- 2 lb (907 g) mirepoix
- Bouquet garni (see Workout 43)

1 Place the bones in the stockpot. Add the cold liquid and bring to a simmer. Remove impurities orany rising fat with a ladle, otherwise the stock will be cloudy.

2 During the last hour add mirepoix and bouquet garni. Simmering extracts the flavors from seasonings.

3 Remove the pot from the heat and strain the stock, which can be used now or chilled for later use (see Workout 42).

42 Workout: Using an ice bath

If you are not going to use the stock immediately, cool it in an ice bath. Take a large container and half-fill it with ice cubes and cold water. After you have strained the stock and poured it into a clean bowl, place the bowl on top of the ice. Continue to fill the container with ice, around the bowl. Stir the stock frequently over the ice bath until it has reached a temperature of 41ºF (5ºC). Skim any fat from the surface. Lift the bowl out, cover it with plastic wrap, label, and place in the refrigerator until it is needed.

43 Workout: Making a bouquet garni

A bouquet garni is a collection of aromatics, the standard being thyme, bay leaf, cracked black peppercorns, and parsley stems. You can wrap everything in a muslin bag or bundle it up in celery stalks or the green tops of leeks.

1 Take a square of muslin and place parsley stems, a bay leaf, black peppercorns, a sprig of thyme, and garlic (optional) on the muslin.

2 Gather up the corners of the muslin.

3 Bunch the muslin to form a bag and tie string around it. The string needs to be long enough to drop the bouquet garni into the stock and tie it to the pot handle.

and body to the finished stock. The best bones to use for a chicken stock are the backbones and the neck.

White fish bones, such as sole, turbot, and whiting, make the best fish stock. Salmon and tuna have too much fat and a too-distinctive flavor. Lamb, turkey, game, and ham bones can also be used to produce stock, but are generally considered too strong in flavor for most dishes.

A mirepoix usually has a ratio of vegetables of 50 percent onions, 25 percent carrots, and 25 percent celery. The sizes of the vegetables are determined by the cooking time of the stock. A beef stock requires whole vegetables or vegetables cut into 1-2 in (2.5-5 cm) pieces, while for chicken or fish the vegetables need to be finely chopped to ½-in (1.2-cm) pieces.

Seasonings are generally added to the stock whole at the beginning of the cooking process. A bouquet garni (usually consisting of a bundle of peppercorns, bay leaves, thyme, and parsley stems, either tied into a muslin bag or wrapped in leeks) is the principal seasoning component of a stock. Salt is never added because the stock is the base for other dishes that will be seasoned by the chef during creation, according to preference. Liquid is the final stock ingredient and cold water is used.

38 | Sauces

The main reasons to add a sauce to food is to add moistness, flavor, and richness, to enhance the food's appearance, and to give it appetite appeal. To make the perfect sauce is the greatest test of any chef, and the ability to pair a sauce with a food shows great understanding of technique and skill. There are two categories of sauce—classic and modern.

Classic sauce method

The "classic" sauce method involves three components; the liquid, or body, of the sauce; the thickening agent; and the addition of seasoning and flavoring ingredients. Most of the famous classic sauces are built on one of five liquids. These are known as the "mother" sauces (see the box below).

Mother sauces

The five mother sauces can be turned into smaller, or derivative, sauces. For example, take hollandaise (awl-lawn-daze), add chopped tarragon and chervil and you have Béarnaise (bare-nez) sauce, then add tomato and you have Choron sauce.

The liquid
• Milk—béchamel (beh-sha-mel)
• White stock (chicken, veal, or fish)—velouté (ve-loo-tay) sauces
• Brown stock—brown sauce, or espagnol
• Tomato with stock—tomato sauce
• Clarified butter—hollandaise

The thickening agents
• Roux (roo) is a cooked mixture of equal quantities of fat and flour by weight. There are three different stages of cooking a roux: white, blond, and brown.
• Starches such as flour, arrowroot, corn flour, or potato starch.
• Vegetable purées.
• Egg yolk and cream liaison. Eggs can thicken a liquid due to the protein in the egg coagulating with heat. The liaison enriches the sauce at the same time as thickening it.
• Reduction. Although not strictly an agent, the process of simmering a sauce reduces the liquid through evaporation and therefore thickens the sauce at the same time as concentrating the flavor.

The seasonings
• Salt is the most important, followed by lemon juice. These two emphasize the flavor that is already there.
• Cayenne and white pepper.
• Madeira and sherry.
• Fresh and dried herbs.

Ingredients in mother sauces

Liquid	+ Thickening agent	= Mother sauce
Milk	+ white roux	= béchamel
White stock (veal, chicken)	+ white or blond roux	= velouté
Brown stock	+ brown roux	= brown sauce
Tomato + stock	+ optional roux	= tomato sauce
Butter	+ egg yolks	= hollandaise

44 Workout: Research mother sauces

Go onto the internet and check out a few of the many culinary sites available—Wikipedia has great culinary sections. Type in "mother sauces" and then see how many variant sauces you can make from one mother sauce. You'll be surprised at the range of sauces available at your fingertips!

45 Workout: Collecting menus

The next time you go out to eat, study the menu and see how many sauces fit into the classic (the five mother sauces) or modern (using light, fresh ingredients) categories. If restaurants permit, collect menus from different venues. If you can't take a menu away, carry a notebook and make notes about the various sauces. This will give you some great ideas to try out at home.

Menus are also a great source of information when it comes to pairing ingredients—especially matching sauces with meats, fish, pastas, or vegetables.

46 Workout: Making different sauces

Try making a roux. The basic formula, by weight, for a roux is three parts flour and two parts fat. Heat the fat in a saucepan over medium heat and add the flour, stirring with a wooden spoon to combine the two. Cook the roux until it is very smooth, with a nice glossy appearance. It should not be too dry or too wet (greasy) and it should have the texture of sand at the beach at low tide. The three stages are white, which is barely colored, blond, which looks like golden straw with a slightly nutty smell, and brown, which is a deep-brown color and strong nutty aroma.

1 Heat the fat over medium heat and add the flour. Stir with a wooden spoon to combine.

2 Blend into a smooth paste to achieve the right consistency. Cook the roux, stirring constantly until the right color and flavor are achieved.

3 Add milk to make a béchamel, white stock to make a velouté, or brown stock to make a brown sauce.

Blonde

White

Brown

Hollandaise sauce
A properly made hollandaise should be smooth, buttery, pale lemon to yellow in color, with a glossy shine and a rich taste. Its texture should be light and frothy with a buttery flavor, but you should also be able to taste the lemon and vinegar.

47 Workout: Finishing a sauce with butter

Monter au beurre *(mohn-tay-ah-burr)* is the process of adding ice-cold whole butter to a sauce to give it additional shine, flavor, and richness. The technique is widely used by chefs to finish small quantities of sauce just before serving.

Using a whisk or spoon, add small cubes of cold butter to the sauce and whip the mixture to blend the butter in. Alternatively you can use a hand blender to finish a sauce with butter.

Modern sauce method

The main modern sauces are: salsa, relish, chutney, flavored oil, and purée, plus a whole range of Asian sauces. The modern sauce method relies less on thickening agents and more on fresher, lighter flavors and ingredients. Today many chefs have also been influenced by cuisines from around the globe, such as Latin American and Asian cuisine. Because of the development of, and experimentation with, new sauces, it is often difficult to classify and define them exactly. Vietnamese, Indian, and Japanese sauces have recently entered the Western chef's repertoire–it would take years of study to know them all.

Relishes are made either using raw or pickled vegetables.

Chutney originated in India and is a cooked fruit and vegetable condiment that is sweet, spicy, and tangy.

Flavored oils make a light and interesting sauce that could be used instead of salad dressings.

Purée. Nearly any vegetable can be turned into a purée, sometimes called a "coulis."

Salsa is the Spanish and Italian word for sauce, but the Mexican salsa is chopped tomatoes, onions, chilies, and herbs. In most English-speaking countries the word "salsa" refers to raw or cooked chopped vegetables, herbs, and occasionally fruits.

Thai dipping sauce
Increasingly popular as a snack or tasty appetizer, Thai sauce with spring rolls is a popular party food to pass around with drinks.

48 Workout: Make pesto

Make your own pesto

Recipe
- 4 oz (120 g) basil leaves
- 4 oz (120 g) toasted pine nuts
- 2 garlic cloves, peeled
- ½ tsp salt
- 4–8 fl oz (120–240 ml) olive oil
- 4 oz (120 g) Parmesan

Put the basil, pine nuts, garlic, and salt in a food processor or pestle and mortar. Grind them together and slowly add the oil until you have thick paste. Taste and adjust seasoning, then stir in the Parmesan.

49 Workout: Pesto serving suggestions

Add extra oil to the pesto, put it in a plastic squeeze bottle and drizzle over grilled meats or fish. Practice a zigzag or complex artistic design on or around the plate to give a rich color and dramatic effect to the presentation of your dish. Alternatively, using a spoon, lightly coat the finished dish or create a pool of sauce, dragging the spoon through it to add visual appeal. Or spoon the sauce under the meat rather than on top. This allows the meat's crust to stay crisp while also offering a contrasting circular shape beneath.

Mango chutney
Chutney, which has its origins in India, is a cooked fruit and vegetable condiment that is sweet, spicy, and tangy. Mango chutney is particularly popular, especially as an accompaniment to curries.

Compound butters

These are made by mixing various seasonings into soft, whole butter. These butters can then be used to add flavor and color to small sauces or served as a sauce in their own right. For example, maître d'hôtel butter (parsley butter) is often served with grilled steak or a piece of fish. It is placed on top just as the dish is served, creating a sauce as the butter melts.

List of compound butters

Butter	Preparation
Anchovy butter	Pound anchovies to a paste and blend with butter.
Caper butter	Add finely chopped capers and anchovies to the butter with a little lemon and orange juice.
Curry butter	Combine curry paste or powder with butter.
Garlic butter	Add finely minced garlic cloves to butter.
Salmon butter	Pound smoked salmon to a paste and blend with butter.
Tomato butter	Add tomato purée to butter.

50 Workout: Making a spicy salsa

Simply mix together the following ingredients for a spicy salsa.

Recipe
- 2–3 medium-sized fresh tomatoes, diced
- ½ red onion, diced
- 1 jalapeño chili pepper, finely diced
- 1 serrano chili pepper, finely diced
- Juice of 1 lime
- ½ cup chopped cilantro
- Salt and pepper to taste
- *Optional:* oregano and/or cumin to taste

51 Workout: Make your own maître d'hôtel butter

You can roll or pipe the butter and serve it with fried/grilled meats or fish.

Recipe
- ½ lb (225 g) butter
- 1 oz (30 g) chopped parsley
- Grated zest and juice of 1 lemon
- Salt and pepper to taste

1 Stir chopped parsley and grated lemon zest into the butter, season with salt and pepper, and stir.

2 Spoon the mixture onto a sheet of waxed paper, creating a log shape. Roll the paper around the butter to create a sausage shape.

3 Compact the butter by rolling and pushing in the ends. Twist the ends firmly and tuck them under. Refrigerate for four hours.

4 To serve the butter, carefully unwrap the roll and slice it into disks, using a sharp knife.

42 | Soups

The word "restaurant" is derived from the first commercial eating places in eighteenth-century France that sold soups to restore (*restaurer*) the French diner.

Soups, or "potages," are technically any blend of meat, fish, and vegetables cooked in a seasoned liquid. They can be served at any time of the day and in any style the chef wishes: hot or cold, creamy or chunky, as an appetizer or as a main course. Soups are a great way to use up your offcuts and a good way of developing your own recipes. They seem to be more popular now than ever before as more and more people are conscious of what they eat. Soups that are made properly can be very nutritious, simple to make, and served as a light meal.

If you have already tried the workouts on stocks and sauces (see pages 36–41), then you have at your disposal the main techniques for making good soups, since you already know how to make a good stock and how to use a roux as a thickening agent.

There are three main categories of soup: clear, or unthickened, soups, thick soups, and specialty soups that may not necessarily fit into the first two groups.

Clear soups

Broths, bouillons, vegetable soups, and consommé all come under the heading "clear." Broths and bouillons are generally clear soups that don't contain any solid ingredients, while vegetable soups are clear, seasoned stock or broth with the addition of one or more vegetables. Sometimes meat or poultry can also be added. Consommé is a completely clear and transparent soup that has been clarified.

Thick soups

Thick soups are heavier than clear soups; they have been thickened using either an agent, such as a roux, or by puréeing one or more of the main ingredients.

Cream, or velouté, soups use a thickening agent such as a roux, beurre manié, or liaison. Purées are soups that use one or two of the main ingredients to thicken the soups, but are not as smooth or creamy as a cream soup. Bisques are made from shellfish and are made like a cream soup, whereas chowders are heavy soups made from fish, shellfish, and vegetables and contain potatoes and milk. "Potage" is a French word that refers to a thick, heavy soup, but it actually also means "soup."

Specialty soups

This category encompasses soups that generally don't fit into the clear or thick soup categories. These could be native to particular countries or regions within countries, such as cold fruit soup, gumbo, hot and sour soup, Russian borscht, or turtle soup.

Garnishes, toppings, and accompaniments

• You can make garnishes from meat, poultry, seafood, pasta, grains, or vegetables.
• Toppings can be anything from fresh herbs, fine julienne or brunoise of vegetables, grated cheese, croutons, sour cream, or crème fraîche.
• Accompaniments can be melba toast, corn chips, cheese straws, wafers, or breadsticks.

Bouillabaise
A classic French peasant soup made with fish, fish stock, and shellfish flavored with saffron.

Soups of the world

Soups are an increasingly significant part of any menu. The sheer variety worldwide is astonishing. This is a list of just a few. Research any cuisine and you'll find an amazing number of soups originating from different countries.

Name	Key ingredients	Country of origin
Borscht	beef, beets, sour cream	Russia
Bouillabaise	fish, shellfish, vegetables	France
Clam chowder	clams, salted pork, fish stock	United States
French onion	onions, brown stock, Gruyère	France
Gumbo	paprika, cayenne, andouille, rice	United States
Hot, sour soup	black mushrooms, rice vinegar	China
Minestrone	white beans, vegetables, Parmesan	Italy
Mulligatawny	curry powder, chicken	India
Pho bo	oxtail, ginger, rice, beef tenderloin	Vietnam
Scotch broth	lamb, barley, parsley	Scotland

52 Workout: Preparing a broth

Broths are often used as a soup base. You can use anything from meat, poultry, fish, grains, and pasta, to legumes, carrots, potatoes, and parsnips, to green vegetables such as peas, spinach, and fresh herbs.

Recipe (Yield: 5 cups/1.1 liters)
• 1 lb (450 g) of one or more main ingredient such as vegetables, meat, poultry, or fish
• 5 cups (1.1 liters) stock
• Salt and pepper
• Cooking oil
• 1 bouquet garni

Cut the vegetables into an even shape and size, add to a large saucepan, and sweat them down with some oil until tender. Add the stock and bring to a simmer, stirring and skimming. Adjust the seasoning throughout the cooking time. Add the main flavoring, if you are using one. You can add onions for French onion soup or meat, poultry, or fish. Add the bouquet garni and cook until the main ingredients are tender. The finished soup should have rich color and deep flavor.

Strawberry soup
Many top restaurants serve sweet soups on their dessert menus. Strawberries, peaches, melon, and raspberries can all make delicious cold soups.

53 Workout: Making a purée soup

This is a great way to use up your vegetable trimmings (though not the skins) and turn them into something that everyone will enjoy. Take a large saucepan and add a small amount of butter or olive oil. Add the trimmings and cook over medium heat to soften them.

1 Add some flour and cook for three to five minutes, stirring to prevent the flour from burning on the bottom of the pan.

2 Pour in some heated vegetable or chicken stock. Bring to a boil and then turn the heat down to a simmer.

3 Cook for 30 minutes or until vegetables are tender. Using a hand blender, blend until the soup is smooth.

4 Pour in some heavy cream (do not boil, otherwise the soup will curdle). Adjust the seasoning if necessary.

5 Add a garnish, as appropriate, and serve.

3

Meat, poultry, fish, & shellfish

One of the most expensive sections of the menu is protein. In this section you will learn how to select the right product from the beginning and how to handle it with care, right through to the end. You will find out what to look for in any kind of protein, whether it is beef, poultry, game, or a delicate piece of shellfish such as fresh scallops. Proteins all have their distinct quality points; find out how they are stored and prepared, right through to their final destination on the plate.

You will also learn the cuts of beef, pork, and lamb, why some cuts of meat are tender and cook easily and quickly, and why others need longer, slower cooking techniques that can develop a rich, delicious sauce to serve the meat in. Find out about the doneness of meat and the difference between wet cooking and dry cooking, to achieve the best possible results. Learn the difference between flat and round fish and how to fabricate them both; how to tell if fresh oysters are really fresh by their shells; how to fabricate fresh, live lobsters, to getting all that scrumptious meat out of the tail and claws of cooked ones. You will be shown the basic cooking methods and which ones are used with certain proteins to cook them to perfection each and every time.

Beef

Cattle have been raised domestically around the world for over 3,000 years, and in many countries beef continues to be the most popular red meat.

Meat is not the only byproduct of cattle; other cattle products are milk, butter, cheese, clothing, leather, and, of course, cattle continue to be used for carrying heavy loads on farms. Kosher beef comes from the forequarter of the animal and can only be butchered and prepared by a *shohet*, a person who is specially trained in removing the veins and arteries. Muslims also follow strict dietary laws and refer to food to be eaten as "halal," or "lawful."

Cattle terminology

"Cattle" is the term used for domestically raised bovines on a farm. Calves are young cattle, the bull is the male calf, and the heifer is the female calf. Bulls are mature, uncastrated males, used for breeding. Steers are male cattle that have been castrated while still young and provide most of the beef people eat, while stags are male cattle that have been castrated after they have matured. Heifers grow into cows, which, fully grown, produce milk.

Meat composition

Meat is the muscle of the animal and it is made up of three components. Whether beef, pork, lamb, or poultry, the makeup is the same: 75 percent water, 20 percent protein, 5 percent fat. Meat also contains vitamins, minerals, and trace amounts of carbohydrates.

Aging

Aging is a natural process that occurs after the animal has been slaughtered. Rigor mortis stiffens the muscles of the animal soon after it has been killed. As the rigor mortis disappears, enzymatic action softens and ripens the tissues of the meat, resulting in flavor and tenderness.

Storing beef

The ideal temperature to store beef is 41°F (5°C). Always store beef in its original wrapping, on a tray, on the lowest shelf of the refrigerator, so that juices do not drip on the floor or contaminate other food. You should use the beef within two to three days of purchase, though if it is vacuum-packed it can last three to four weeks provided it is unopened.

Timeless flavors

Beef can stand up to many strong flavors, from horseradish when roasted to pesto when grilled, chili powder in a stew or braised, to Indian seasoning in a curry. Cuts from the tenderloin marry well with hollandaise sauce or a rich Madeira sauce.

The main cuts
Beef is split through the backbone into sides. The sides are divided between the twelfth and thirteenth ribs into forequarters and hindquarters. Study this illustration and learn the major cuts.

Grades of beef

• Specialty beef, such as Kobe beef from Japan, Limousin beef from France, certified Angus, natural, organic, and dry-aged beef are all available and come in different grades.
• Prime is the highest-quality and most expensive beef on the market. It has very nice marbling because of the feeding practices of the farmers, is extremely juicy and full of flavor, and is very costly and limited in supply.
• Choice is the most-used beef in restaurants and hotels and is a high-quality product, excellent value for money, very juicy and tender, and widely available at any time of the year.
• Select has limited marbling, is very lean, and acceptable.
• Standard lacks marbling and is low-quality meat.
• Commercial comes from older animals and is tough.
• Utility, cutter, and canner, are very low in quality and are used for canned meat products. They are rarely used in the food service industry.

54 Workout: Stages of beef doneness

Practice cooking steaks to each level of doneness. Always sear the meat with high heat to create a desirable flavor and color. Brown the surface first, then cook the meat.

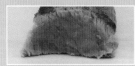

Rare: Brown surface, thin layer of gray cooked meat, red interior.

Medium: Brown surface, thicker layer of gray cooked meat, pink interior.

Well done: Brown surface, cooked throughout (gray) interior.

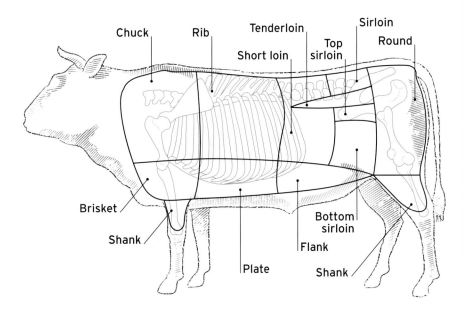

Chuck · Rib · Tenderloin · Short loin · Top sirloin · Sirloin · Round · Brisket · Shank · Plate · Flank · Bottom sirloin · Shank

55 Workout: Preparing and portioning beef tenderloin

The tenderloin is one of the most expensive cuts of meat, so you should take extra care and attention to remove the silver skin and leave the meat as intact as possible. The tenderloin contains several sections: the chain or long side muscle, the large side muscle, and the main center-cut section.

1 Cut and pull the excess fat from the tenderloin to expose the meat. Then remove the chain of loose meat that runs its length.

2 Once you have trimmed excess fat, start to trim the silver skin. Insert your boning knife just under this sinew.

3 Hold the silver skin with your fingers and slide your knife underneath, keeping it tight. This way your knife is not cutting into the meat.

4 Glide your knife all the way up the tenderloin, keeping it against the silver skin, and proceed to remove all the sinew.

5 Once the tenderloin is free of fat and sinew, cut the meat into usable portions, starting with the head (the chateaubriand).

6 Cut the remaining piece into two portions, then into fillet steaks, tournedos, medallions, and tips.

7 To cut tournedos, slice the meat into 1-in (2.5-cm) widths. For medallions cut thinner. Use the tips for stir-fries or beef stroganoff.

Degrees of doneness

The term "doneness" of meat depends whether the meat was cooked by dry or wet heat.

Dry-heat cooking is when the meat's internal temperature has reached a certain degree. As red meat cooks, the color of the meat changes. This indicates the degree of doneness.

- Very rare   115ºF–120ºF (46ºC–49ºC)
- Rare   125ºF–130ºF (52ºC–54ºC)
- Medium rare   130ºF–140ºF (54ºC–60ºC)
- Medium   140ºF–150ºF (60ºC–66ºC)
- Medium well   155ºF–165ºF (68ºC–74ºC)
- Well done   Above 165ºF (74ºC)

Wet-heat cooking is when the connective tissues have been broken down enough to make the meat tender, by stewing or braising.

56 Workout: Carving roast beef

Allow the beef to rest after removing from the oven, to allow the juices to remain in the structure of the meat while you carve it.

1 Place the joint on a chopping board and begin by removing the forerib, making sure you keep your knife by the bone.
2 Glide down the bone with your knife, cutting away until the bone has been removed.
3 Moving the knife back and forth, in a smooth motion, carve the meat into thick, even slices.
4 Perfectly cooked beef should be rare, but this can be tricky to carve. Just take your time.

1

2

3

4

48 Pork

Pork comes from pigs that are aged between six months and one year. It is a very popular meat, with several hundred different breeds worldwide, but only a small percentage is actually consumed fresh. Most pork is processed into bacon, cooked ham, cured ham, sausage, pâtés, and byproducts such as lard.

Trichinosis

Trichinosis is a disease caused by a parasite that lives in the muscle tissue of hogs and some wild animals. This disease is not found in English or American pigs these days, but it can be found in other countries. This parasite is killed at a temperature of 137°F (58°C), but to be safe, pork should be cooked to at least 150°F–155°F (66°C–68°C), which is in the medium- to well-done range. Most people prefer pork to be cooked to 160°F (71°C).

Cuts of pork
Get to know the prime cuts of the pig and their uses. A good chef should be able to break a pig down into its major cuts; a great chef will be able to use every part of the pig on the menu, from snout to tail.

Storing pork

As with any meat, check the temperature on delivery. Pork should be 41°F (5°C) or below, and it should be stored at that temperature. Just like beef, pork should be stored wrapped on a tray and placed on the lowest shelf in the refrigerator to prevent cross-contamination with other foods.

Freshness

Pork should be pink to reddish in color, the fat should be white, there should be no perceptible odor, and the flesh should be firm and not too dry or too wet. If the flesh is dark in color, brown, purple, or even green with black spots, if the fat is sticky, or if there is a sour smell, discard the meat immediately.

Timeless flavors

Pork benefits from a heavy layer of fat and good marbling. Robust flavors can be used on fresh pork joints and cuts, such as garlic, and strong earthy herbs, such as rosemary, thyme, and marjoram. Pork is ideal for barbecuing and serving either with vinegar-based or mustard-based barbecue sauce, along with corn and rice. Barbecuing with Asian flavors is also very popular, using such ingredients as ginger, lemongrass, sesame oil, and soy sauce. Leaner cuts from the loin go well with mustard, tarragon, and mild cream sauces. Roast pork with

crackling, served with apples and a rich gravy, is an excellent dish for Sunday dinner.

The term charcuterie (*shar-COO-tuhr-ree*) refers to the cooking of pig flesh or pork and the charcutière is a specially trained chef who prepares these items. Unlike beef, aging is unnecessary as the flesh is naturally tender and firm, and it has an even covering of fat.

Processed pork

Processing is the act of changing food by artificial means; 70 percent of all pork is processed. The most common processing methods are curing or smoking to produce bacon, ham, and other food items.

Cured pork holds its flavor longer than fresh pork and has a longer shelflife. There are two

57 Workout: Slicing sausage

Cured sausages are served sliced in a traditional platter of charcuterie and make an excellent starter or appetizer. Practice slicing a variety of sausage types to perfect your technique.

Holding your serrated knife in one hand and the sausage in the other, slowly carve back and forth to cut it into thin, even slices.

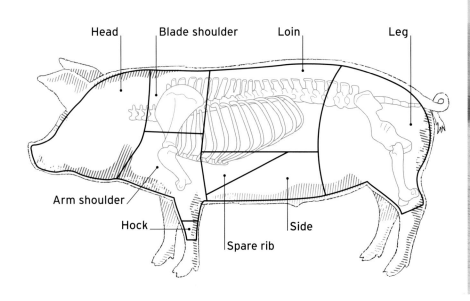

Head   Blade shoulder   Loin   Leg

Arm shoulder

Hock

Spare rib

Side

methods of curing pork–dry and wet. Dry is the oldest method, involving rubbing salt and seasoning over the surface of the pork, then covering the meat completely with salt and storing in the refrigerator until it absorbs the seasoning and dries the meat out.

Wet-curing uses salt, sugar, spices, flavorings, nitrites, and water to preserve the meat. Pickled curing involves submerging the pork in brine, which is a mixture of water, salt, and other seasonings, until the solution penetrates into the center of the meat. Injection-curing uses the same brine but injects the solution into the pork for a faster method of curing. Sugar-curing involves covering the pork with brine that has been sweetened with sugar or molasses.

Smoking is also used to process pork, add flavor, and give a longer shelflife. The pork is usually brined first, dried, then smoked with hardwoods such as hickory, apple, or cherry wood to give its distinctive flavor.

There are several types of spicy sausage. Andouille *(an-DOO-ee)* is a spicy smoked pork sausage, while mortadella *(mohr-tah-DEH-lah)* is an Italian smoked sausage made with beef, pork, and pork fat flavored with cilantro. Chorizo is a Spanish spicy sausage used in classic paella.

58 Workout: Preparing pork lardons

Pork lardons come from the belly cut of the pig. They are full of flavor because of the high amount of fat around the meat.

1 Remove the skin from the bacon with your chef's knife, then slice the meat into $^2/_5$-in (1-cm) thick strips.
2 Repeat the process along the entire length of the bacon, aiming to keep every slice the same thickness.
3 Turn the slice of bacon 90 degrees and continue to cut into $^2/_5$-in (1-cm) lardon pieces.

59 Workout: Preparing a tenderloin

Tenderloin of pork is the tenderest part of the pig. It is cheap and easy to cook and it blends well with many flavors and seasonings. It can be cooked whole or sliced into steaks or cubes to make kabobs. The first thing you need to do is remove the tough, chewy membrane that will distort the shape of the meat as it cooks.

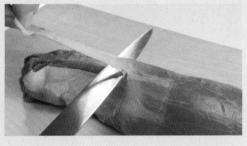

1 Place the tenderloin on the chopping board and pat it dry to remove any moisture. This will make it easier to handle.

2 Using a boning knife or your chef's knife, hook the tip of the knife under the sinew and cut slightly underneath it.

3 Hold the sinew with your fingers, keeping it taut. This will allow the knife to remove the sinew and not much flesh. The sinew will disappear. Simply cut through at this point and the sinew will come away from the meat. Remove all the sinew.

4 Start at the tail end of the tenderloin and remove any leftover sinew or fat as you work your way to the head of the tenderloin.

5 Now the tenderloin is free of sinew and fat you can leave it whole to roast or grill, or you can cut it into steaks for sautéeing.

6 The tenderloin head is too thin to cut into an even-size steak, so turn your knife 90 degrees and cut against the grain.

7 Rest the meat, so that the cut of the meat faces upward. This makes it easier to season and handle for storage.

50 Lamb & mutton

Lamb tends to be fatty, with a distinctive flavor, coming in five grades: prime, choice, good, utility, and cull. It is commonly used in Middle Eastern cuisine, but is also popular in Europe.

Preparation

Lamb or mutton is very often covered with a substantial amount of fat, which should be trimmed before cooking. Lamb fat melts very quickly when it is heated and it tends to have an acute woolly or musty taste. This means that the more fat you remove prior to cooking, the better the result will be.

In order for meat to be called "lamb," it has to come from a sheep, of either sex, that is less than 12 months of age before it is slaughtered. Mutton is usually over 16 months old before being slaughtered and compared to lamb it has a strong flavor and a tougher texture. Mutton is rarely available in the United States unless it is obtained via a Middle Eastern food market. It can be used in any lamb recipe that calls for a longer cooking time, as this is needed to tenderize the mature meat.

The average weight of lamb is normally 65 lb (29.5 kg); spring lamb is smaller, usually under 50 lb (22 kg) and has been milk-fed. In France, lamb falls into three categories: milk lamb, butchered about 30 days before being weaned; white lamb (the most common available in late December through to June); and grazing lamb, which is six to nine months old and has been pasture-grazed.

Demand for lamb

Lamb is very popular in the United Kingdom, with Welsh lamb being the best choice a chef can buy, whereas in the United States lamb accounts for a very small percentage of meat sales. Although American demand for lamb is not great, most lamb is imported from New Zealand and Australia as domestic lamb production cannot meet United States consumer demands. Because of the age of lamb, the meat is very tender and, like pork, does not need to be aged. Chefs can use any cooking method on lamb and marry it with robust sauces and accompaniments because of its strong, distinctive flavor.

Storing lamb

Lamb should be light red in color, and the fat white, with no unpleasant odor. The meat should be firm, without any slimy or dry areas. Lamb, like all meats, should be kept at 41°F (5°C),

60 Workout: Butterflying a leg of lamb

Butterflying a leg of lamb is an essential skill that you, as a chef, will need to know. If you are not roasting the leg whole, removing the bone will make the meat more manageable to cut into steaks, to grill, or dice for kabobs or stews. You need to use your boning knife for this procedure.

1 Hold your boning knife, like a dagger, in one hand. With your other hand, hold the bone and start to ease the meat away from it.

2 Keep the tip of the knife against the bone and start to open the thickest part of the leg.

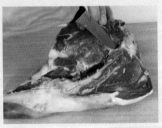

3 Keep your knife tight against the bone, bearing in mind its shape, and make confident movements, working around it.

4 Gradually remove the bone and keep it to be used for making stock.

5 Now concentrate on opening the whole leg up, with long, shallow incisions into the flesh.

6 Holding the knife in the normal way, trim any fat and sinew away from the flesh.

7 The finished product should be an even piece of meat, ready to be cut into steaks, dice, or placed in a marinade to grill.

or lower if possible, and stored wrapped on a tray on the bottom shelf in the refrigerator, to prevent cross-contamination with other foods. Fresh lamb spoils very easily and should be used within three to five days of purchase, unless it is vacuum-packed, which will allow it to be stored for longer. You should discard lamb if it looks brown; if the fat has turned soft and yellow in appearance; or if the meat is dry or slimy to the touch, and the odor is strong and acidic.

Timeless flavors

Its subtleness and elegance makes lamb a perfect meat for fresh herbs and aromatics as well as exotic flavors. Lamb and mint sauce is a classic dish served in Great Britain, Australia, and New Zealand. Rosemary, garlic, and oregano go well with lamb's pronounced flavor. Vinegar is used in many preparations with lamb to balance out the fattiness of the meat. In Greece and Italy lamb is combined with citrus fruits, wine, and yogurt to brighten the flavor of lamb stews. The North African tagine dish uses dried fruits and root vegetables, while in Indian cuisine, lamb is a popular component of curries.

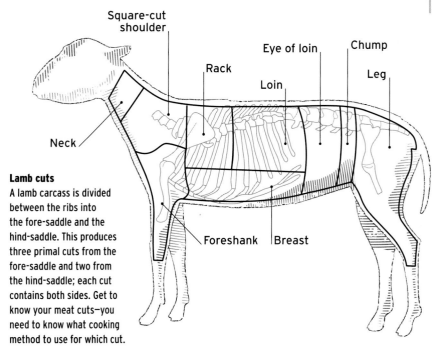

Lamb cuts
A lamb carcass is divided between the ribs into the fore-saddle and the hind-saddle. This produces three primal cuts from the fore-saddle and two from the hind-saddle; each cut contains both sides. Get to know your meat cuts—you need to know what cooking method to use for which cut.

---

61 Workout: Frenching a rack of lamb

You can order ready-prepared French racks from your meat supplier, but this technique shows great knife skills, and once you have mastered it you will never forget how to do it.

1 Use your boning knife to cut through the fat, all the way to the bone. Your first cut should be about 1 in (3 cm) from the eye of the meat.

2 Hold the fat with one hand and start to pull it back as your knife hand slices the fat in long even strokes, keeping the knife on the bone.

3 Use the tip of the knife to score the thin membrane between each rib and then cut through to remove the fat between each bone.

4 Take your time and scrape down each bone, removing as much fat and sinew as possible, to leave the bone as clean as you can.

5 Trim the thick layer of fat from the rack, gently slice your knife through the fatty tissue, and pull the covering back with your free hand.

6 Once you have removed the thick layer of fat, gently remove any excess fat, but leave a thin coating to protect the meat as it cooks.

---

62 Workout: Carving a leg of lamb

You will need a chopping board, carving knife or chef's knife, and a carving fork to successfully carve a leg of lamb.

1 Start at the far end of the leg and carve as many thin slices as possible before you come across the bone.

2 Proceed farther down the leg and cut a "V" shape, like a wedge, into the leg.

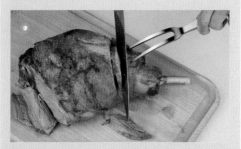

3 Continue carving down the leg and placing each slice on the chopping board as you go.

Types of game

- The blackbuck antelope is about half the size of a large deer, has no body fat, and should be cooked in the same manner as venison.
- Bison (American buffalo) are raised like beef cattle and have meat full of flavor. It may be prepared in the same manner as lean beef (see page 46).
- The deer family includes elk, moose, reindeer, red-tailed deer, and white-tailed deer, and the meat from the deer family is known as "venison." The most popular cuts are from the loin, leg, and rack. The loin can be roasted, sautéed, or grilled to medium rare. The leg and rack are usually marinated and braised or stewed.
- Rabbit has a mild, lean, and tender flesh, and its flavor and texture are similar to chicken. The average weight of a rabbit is 2 ½–3 lb (1.2–1.4 kg). Hares can weigh up to 14 lb (6.3 kg) and have lean, dark, strong-flavored meat that is good for stewing. Rabbits can be roasted, pan-fried, stewed, or braised.
- Wild boar is a close relative of the hog family with a leaner, stronger flavor. Wild boar can be used in recipes for venison and pork.
- Pheasant is the most popular of the game birds. It has a mild flavor and is excellent to roast, stew, or braise. The carcass makes an excellent stock that can be used to make consommé or a rich sauce. A bird normally weighs around 2 lb 4 oz (1 kg) and serves two people.
- Partridge has a less-delicate flavor than pheasant and the meat tends to be tougher. It can be roasted or cut into pieces to be sautéed or braised.
- Quail is related to the pheasant family and can be stuffed and served whole or breasts removed and grilled, roasted, broiled, or sautéed. Quails are very small, the breast meat weighing only 1-2 oz (30-60 g).

Game

The term "game" refers to animals that have been hunted for sport or food. Traditionally game supplies have depended on the season and the hunter's success. The increase in the popularity of game because of consumer desires for leaner, healthier meats has led to farm-raising and animal husbandry to supply that demand. Free roaming and domesticated wild animals fall into the category of "game."

Game is categorized into "large" and "small." The most popular of the large variety is venison. This is a really lean, dark meat, red in color, suitable for roasting, grilling, and sautéeing. Smaller game is usually rabbit or hare, which is mild in taste and has a fine, textured meat structure. Feathered game covers quail, which is the most popular, followed by pheasant, partridge, woodcock, and ratites (ostrich, emu, and rhea).

Purchasing game

Furred game meats are available fresh or frozen. Game birds are available cleaned and boned, fresh or frozen. Just like any other meat that you would purchase, check that the flesh is firm, without any slime or "off" odor. As with any other meat, it should be wrapped and refrigerated at 41°F (5°C) or below. Fresh game used to be hung so that the meat could mature, or age, but commercially sold game is generally fully aged and ready to use when delivered.

Preparing game

Tradition has always called for game to be marinated in a mixture of red wine, berries, herbs, and spices. Commercially raised game does not necessarily need to be marinated, since the meat tends to come from young, tender animals that have a milder flavor than their wild cousins.

Wild and domestic
Game can be further classified as "wild" or "domestic." Wild game inhabits its native environment and is hunted for personal consumption by hunters. Domestic game is raised in a farm environment and can be purchased throughout the year.

63 Workout:
How to truss a game bird

Game birds have less fat than other poultry, so they easily dry out during cooking. They are always trussed so that they cook evenly and are barded with a layer of fat, which gives moisture and flavor. The fat is trussed to the top of the game bird, covering the breasts. This gives the bird a protective layer of fat that stops it from becoming dry during roasting. To truss, start by wrapping the twine around the knuckles of the leg bones. Then bring the twine toward the front of the bird, between each breast and thigh, then around to the front of the breasts, and tie. This will truss the bird so that it cooks evenly. Follow Workout 65 for barding.

64 Workout: Jointing a rabbit

Rabbits are small, burrowing animals that have been raised domestically for many years as part of the food chain. You can buy them fresh or frozen, either whole or portioned. It is not too difficult to fabricate a whole rabbit. All you need is a clean chopping board and a chef's knife.

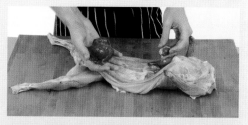

1 Start by placing the rabbit on its back and removing the kidneys and liver from the belly cavity (these are edible and can be used in pâtés or terrines).

Timeless flavors

Game has such an assertive flavor that it can benefit from fruits such as apricots, blueberries, cranberries, peaches, pears, raspberries, or plums. These have a tart sweetness that complements its flavor.

2 Pull back the hind legs to expose the joint. Then, using your chef's knife, remove the hind legs by cutting close to the backbone and through the joint on the other side.

3 Pull the foreleg away from the body, then remove the leg by cutting beneath the shoulder blades. Repeat this process on the other side.

4 Cut through the breastbone and open up the ribcage. Separate the flesh from the rib bones and remove the bones.

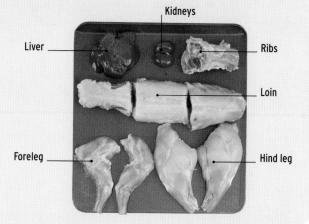

Kidneys

Liver ———

——— Ribs

——— Loin

Foreleg ———

——— Hind leg

5 Cut the loin into the required number of portions. You should have eight sections, along with the liver and kidneys.

65 Workout: How to bard a game bird

You have already trussed the game bird; now it is time to bard it. The fat you use can be the back fat from pork or streaky bacon—both will give moisture, flavor, and protection to the delicate breast of the game bird.

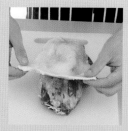

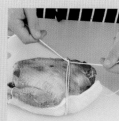

1 Cover the breast of the bird with a thin layer of fat or bacon.

2 Take a piece of twine and wrap it around the bird, securing the fat with a simple knot.

3 Wrap another piece of twine around the breasts and turn the bird over. Secure with another knot.

4 Now the bird is ready for the oven.

54 Poultry

The term "poultry" refers to any domesticated bird used for human consumption, and it is one of the most popular items on the menu. There are six classifications of poultry: chicken, turkey, duck, goose, guinea fowl, and pigeon.

Chicken and turkey

It is said that a great chef is measured by his ability to roast a perfect chicken. This might seem an easy task, but the structure of a chicken challenges even the most experienced chef: tender breasts that only need a little heat to keep them moist and succulent, to legs and thighs that are compact, sinewy and require longer cooking to reach doneness. Every chef has a personal way to roast a chicken, but buying from a local farm that raises its chickens organically is the best way to start, and perfecting the roasting technique comes with practice. The best to buy are small birds. Because of demand you can buy turkeys all year round, though mostly frozen. Fresh turkeys are available in abundance during the holidays.

Duck and goose

Buying from your local farmer is the best way to buy fresh ducks and geese, since buying from a commercial source usually means buying frozen. Similar to a chicken, the duck breast has richer meat, while the legs are more tender. Roast duck is delicious, but many chefs prefer to cook the breast separately from the legs to keep them rare and moist, while the legs make great confit. A goose produces plenty of meat and is enjoyed by many during festive seasons.

Guinea fowl and pigeon

A relative of the chicken and partridge, the guinea fowl is small, dark-fleshed, gamey in flavor, and the flesh is quite dry. To retain moistness you may find that you need to bard the bird when roasting. The pigeon, on the other hand, is small, firm-fleshed, and very tender.

Goose and peas
As well as roasting, goose can be slow-cooked in a casserole.

Poultry accompaniments

The versatility of poultry may account for its popularity among chefs and home cooks alike. When roasted, all it takes is a simple rub with salt, black pepper, and olive oil. You can make gravy from its juices or chicken-based velouté sauces scented with fresh herbs, lemon, and cracked black pepper—these are common accompaniments that enhance the pure flavor of the poultry.

You can use wet or dry marinates with any poultry; apply marinates made with garam masala, or other spicy blends, just before roasting, grilling, or stewing to make that perfect dish that everyone will enjoy.

Purchasing and storing poultry

You can buy poultry in many forms: fresh or frozen, whole or cut up, bone in or boneless, portion-controlled (PC), individually quick-frozen (IQF), or ground. Poultry is a potentially hazardous food and is highly susceptible to contamination by salmonella bacteria. Fresh chicken and other fresh birds should be stored on ice at 32°F–34°F (0°C –2°C) for two to four days after purchase. Frozen birds should be kept at 0°F (-18°C) , or below, for up to six months. Never attempt to cook poultry that is still partially frozen.

66 Workout: Removing a chicken breast

The first thing to do is to remove the wishbone at the neck. This is easily done by inserting your knife into the neck cavity and scraping it down the bone to loosen it. You then use your fingers to pull the wishbone out.

1 Feel with your fingers along the breastbone. Place your chef's knife on one side of the bone and cut through the flesh.

2 Keeping your knife to the bone, carefully cut through the meat until you have removed it from the carcass.

67 Workout: Skinning and slicing

Chicken is a very lean meat to use, but to remove more saturated fat from the bird, you can remove the skin, making it even healthier for you or your customers.

1 Hold the breast at the thickest part and pull the skin away from the meat in the opposite direction.

2 Using your chef's knife, cut the breast into the required number of slices and thickness.

68 Workout: Cutting an eight-way chicken

Cutting a chicken into even-sized portions is a great skill that an aspiring chef needs to know. Also it is much cheaper for you to cut up a chicken than to buy it in ready-prepared portions. You can also use the bones for stock.

1 Place the chicken on your chopping board and, using your knife or a pair of poultry shears or scissors, remove any trussing string from the chicken.

2 Turn the chicken over and remove the rump of the bird. This is the fatty piece of meat and skin at the opposite end to the neck cavity.

3 Using your knife, cut along the backbone, through the skin. Do not cut through the bones, only the skin.

4 Using your fingers, pull back the skin from the bones. Then, using your paring knife, release the oysters from their sockets. These are located at the base of each leg.

5 Turn the chicken over and pull back the skin on the breast. Then cut through the skin between the breast and leg. Repeat for the other leg.

6 Dislocate the leg joints from the main carcass by twisting both legs out of the sockets at the same time.

7 Using your knife, remove the leg completely from the main carcass. You should not be cutting through any bone, only releasing the skin.

8 Open the leg up and cut though the ball and socket joint of the leg. This will give you two pieces of meat, known as the thigh and drumstick.

9 Now that the legs are removed, use your scissors and cut along the bones from the side of the chicken and also remove the backbone. Keep these bones to make chicken stock.

10 Place the crown of the chicken flat on the board and, using your knife, slice through the skin and flesh on either side of the breastbone until you hit the bones.

11 Using your scissors, cut through the bone from top to bottom of the crown, leaving you with two equal-sized portions

12 Hold the wing with one hand and, with your knife hand, cut through the breast meat at an angle.

13 Cut through the bone, giving two portions of breast meat. Repeat on the other breast.

14 You should have eight equal portions of chicken: two drum sticks, two thighs, two wings with breast meat, and two breasts.

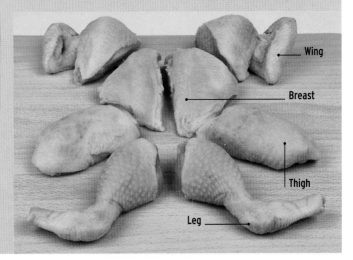

Wing

Breast

Thigh

Leg

Fish

Fish, or *poisson*, are found in both fresh and salt water. There are thousands of varieties worldwide, though many are now on the endangered list because of overfishing and damage caused by polluted waters. This makes it very important for you, as a chef, to learn how and where to buy fish, so that fishing sustainability can be maintained.

Healthy option

Populations of countries such as Japan, China, and Scandinavia consume large amounts of fish in their diet and seem to benefit from low rates of heart disease and many cancers, compared to countries that do not eat much fish at all. Scientific studies suggest that omega-3, found in fatty fish such as salmon, trout, and tuna, have many health benefits for those who eat them regularly.

The main parts

Fish have four main parts: the head, the body, the tail, and the fins. If the fish is not served whole to your customer, then it is normal practice to bring just the body to the table. The bones, tail, fins, and cleaned head are normally used to make fish stock or they are used as a seasoning for soups.

Most fish are very low in cholesterol, consisting of 70 percent water, 10 to 20 percent protein, and only about 1 percent fat, plus traces of vitamins A, B, and other minerals. Fish are very low in calories (Kcal): approximately 160 Kcal per 4 oz (120 g) for fatty fish, such as salmon, and 70 Kcal for lean fish, such as sole.

Buying fish

With increased speed and safety of shipping and transporting fish, it is now readily available almost everywhere. Since fish found at the local fish market may not be local or regional, it is very important that you know how to identify freshly caught fish and how to store it correctly.

Handling fish

You should handle fish carefully, because it is one of the most perishable foods you will deal with as a chef. It should be stored at a temperature of 30°F (-1°C) on crushed ice, with

Wash the whole fish under cold, running water, then pat dry with a paper towel. Place the fish on your chopping board and carefully clean it with a paper towel on both sides. This will remove any blood or dirt and also dry the fish, stopping it from moving around on the chopping board as you remove the fillets.

a drip tray underneath to allow the ice to drain. Cover the container or store it in a separate fridge, away from other foods, if possible.

Drawing

Draw a whole fish (remove the innards) as soon as possible after you purchase it because the entrails will quickly deteriorate and start to decompose the flesh. You should use fish immediately after purchase or store it for between one and two days only before use.

Storing and freezing

Store frozen fish at 0°F (-18°C). You can freeze flat fish for up to two months and round fish for up to six months. Label all fish and wrap it well to prevent freezer-burn. Thaw the fish in the refrigerator for between 18 to 36 hours, depending on its size, before you prepare and cook it.

Flatfish

Flatfish swim through the water horizontally and spend most of their time resting flat on the ocean floor. The three most common varieties are sole, halibut, and flounder. Flatfish generally have dark skin on top and a white underside. They have two eyes on the top of the head and a backbone that runs through the center of the body. The fish is composed of two thin layers of flesh (meat) or "fillets" on either side. These can either be served whole or removed and served as individual portions.

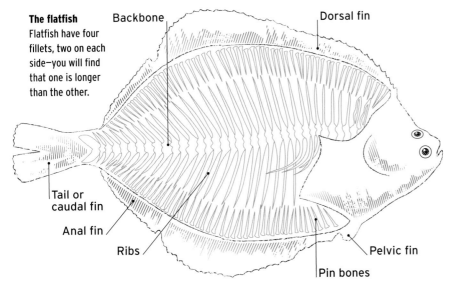

The flatfish
Flatfish have four fillets, two on each side—you will find that one is longer than the other.

Backbone

Dorsal fin

Tail or caudal fin

Anal fin

Ribs

Pelvic fin

Pin bones

Fish freshness checklist

Characteristics	Fresh	Not so fresh
Smell	of the sea–fresh	ammonia–fishy
Eyes	clear, bright, full	sunken, cloudy
Scales	plentiful, shiny, tight	loose, dry
Flesh texture	firm, elastic	soft, leaves marks
Grills	bright red or pink	gray or brown

70 Workout: Filleting a flatfish

1 Place the sole on the chopping board and score with a knife down the backbone.

Before you begin, run your finger down the backbone, which runs down the center of the fish. This is where you will make your first cut to remove the fillets. Just like butchering meat, always keep your knife close to the bone. Take off as much of the meat as possible, remembering that the more flesh left on the bone, the more the edible piece of fish will cost.

2 Make sure you get all the flesh from beside the head by gently gliding your knife from head to tail.

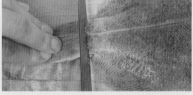

3 At the tail end of the fish, cut through the skin to the bone. This will make removing the fillet easier.

4 Using your fingers, pull back the flesh as you slice through the fillet; this will ease removing the fillet.

5 Take your time and gently slide the knife all the way down the fillet. Keep your knife close to the bones.

6 Lightly place the heel of your hand on the head of the fish while you pull the fillet away from the fins.

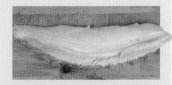

7 Once you have removed one fillet, repeat the process until all four fillets have been removed.

71 Workout: Removing the skin

If you are frying or deep-frying the fillet, leave the skin on, since this will hold the fillet together. If you are poaching the fillet, then you really need to remove the skin. Your filleting knife, with its flexible blade, is the ideal tool for this job.

1 Sprinkle a little salt on the tail of the fillet; this will make it easier to grip as you remove the skin.

2 Keep your knife at a 25-degree angle and, using a firm sawing motion back and forth, slowly take your knife up the fillet.

3 Tightly hold the skin and continue to slice your knife up the fillet until you have removed the flesh.

Round fish

As the name suggests, these fish are round in shape and they swim through the water in a vertical position. They have one eye on either side of the head, which can be round, compressed, or oval in shape. The backbone of a round fish runs along the upper edge of the body. Popular round fish include cod, trout, salmon, and haddock.

A good chef knows how to break down and fabricate whole fish. If you have already tried the workouts on flatfish (see pages 56–57), then you are well on your way to becoming an all-round chef, since many establishments no longer break down fish if they can save money buying in ready-prepared portions. However, many top restaurants and hotels still require chefs to fabricate onsite.

Portion size

There is considerable loss during the cleaning and portioning of fish, as the edible portion may be only 40 percent of the original weight of the whole fish. Thirty percent is lost when you remove the internal organs, while the head, skin, and bones may account for a further 20 to 30 percent. Portion size when your customer receives it is generally a 6½–8½ oz (180–240 g) entrée serving.

Buying fish

If you buy the fish whole, it has its internal organs intact. If the fish is in this form it has a very short shelflife and needs your skill to fabricate, prepare, and serve it as soon as possible. High-end establishments purchase whole fish so that chefs can fabricate them in the kitchen and use the bones to make fresh stock for soups and sauces.

If you buy the fish drawn, you buy the whole fish, but with the internal organs removed, along with the gills, fins, scales, and sometimes the head. Drawn fish have the longest shelflife and many food service establishments purchase them in this form.

Preparation

A round fish provides two fillets, one from each side. The fillet may have the skin on or it may have been removed. Fillets are the most popular market form of purchase and many food service establishments buy them like this.

If the fish has been "butterflied" it has been dressed and cut open like a butterfly, with the skin still attached. Fish "steaks" are cross-sectional cuts of dressed fish, usually with the skin left on and the backbone intact. Fish "cubes" are used for kabobs, fish stews, and soups, and usually come from leftover pieces of a large fish.

Frozen fish terms

Fresh	never frozen
Chilled	held at 30°F–34°F (-1°C–1°C)
Flash-frozen	frozen onboard ship, within hours of being caught
Fresh-frozen	frozen while still fresh, but not as fast as flash-frozen
Frozen	subject to temperatures of 0°F (-18°C) or lower, to preserve quality
Glazed	dipped in iced water to form a glaze to protect from freezer-burn
Fancy	previously frozen

72 Workout: Scaling

Use the back of your chef's knife to remove the scales from the fish. The best way to do this is to hold the tail of the fish in one hand and the knife at an angle to the fish in the other hand. Always scrape backward against the fish, starting at the tail and moving up to the head.

Fabricating fish

When fabricating always remove the gills from the head if you are serving the fish whole or if you are using the head and bones for stock. This is because the gills will impart a bitter taste. You can leave the head on whole fish since this makes it easier to turn it during cooking; it also contributes to the presentation of the finished dish. The head of large, round fish offers tasty treats, particularly from the cheeks.

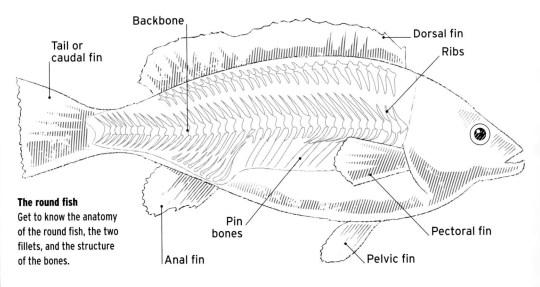

The round fish
Get to know the anatomy of the round fish, the two fillets, and the structure of the bones.

Backbone

Tail or caudal fin

Dorsal fin

Ribs

Pin bones

Anal fin

Pectoral fin

Pelvic fin

73 Workout: Drawing round fish

Before cooking a whole fish or filleting any fish, you need to remove the intestines first. Make sure you clean the fish and also your chopping board, so that you are not transferring bacteria.

1 Place one hand on the fish and, using the tip of your filleting knife, score through the skin from the anal vent to the fins just before the gills.

2 Open up the vent and remove the intestines in one movement. You may want to wear a pair of gloves at this stage.

3 Holding the intestines at the head, use a pair of scissors to snip the connection and discard the intestines. Wash and dry the fish before processing further.

74 Workout: Skinning and filleting monkfish

Monkfish has two fillets, one on either side of the backbone, which runs from the rather large head to the small tail. It is a delicious, dense meaty fish that marries well with most flavors, such as a rich tomato sauce served with fresh pasta or lightly grilled or roasted and served with olive oil and lime juice with a freshly made salad. Monkfish has no scales, so all you need to do is make sure you wash any sea slime off the fish before you start to work on it.

1 Pull the dorsal fin away from the fish and, using a pair of kitchen scissors, snip it off.

2 Pull back the skin and, using your filleting knife, gently cut through any membrane.

3 Hold the top of the fish with the heel of your hand and pull the skin back with the other hand.

4 Feel where the backbone starts and release the flesh from the bone.

5 Remove the fillets and any thin membrane that might still be on the flesh.

6 Cut into even-sized portions for grilling, roasting, or pan-frying.

75 Workout: Filleting

Filleting a round fish is very similar to filleting a flatfish. You need to remember to keep your filleting knife as close to the bones as possible. To remove the pin bones you will need a good pair of fish tweezers, which will make the job a lot easier.

1 Start by removing the pectoral fins and dorsal fins from the fish with your kitchen scissors.

2 Make your first incision just behind the pectoral fins, on a diagonal, on one side of the fish. Cut through until you feel the backbone of the fish and stop.

3 Turn the fish around and score down the backbone, keeping it as close to the bone as possible. Pull back the flesh and make a long, sweeping motion from the head to the tail.

4 You can now insert the knife all the way through one side of the fish.

5 Place one hand on the fish and move your knife along the backbone. Release the fillet.

6 Use your knife to remove the belly flap from the fillet and your tweezers to remove any pin bones.

60 Shellfish

Shellfish have shells that protect their bodies, but they do not have either internal skeletons or backbones. They can be divided into three separate categories: mollusks, crustaceans, and cephalopods.

Nutritious and tasty
Seafood is an excellent source of protein.

Types of shellfish

Mollusks have a soft, segmented body enclosed in a shell. They are divided into two sub-categories: bivalves and univalves. Bivalves (oysters, mussels, and clams) have two shells, one on top and one on the bottom, with a hinge holding them together. Univalves (periwinkles, abalone, and conch) have only one shell and are classed as marine snails. They have a single foot with which to attach themselves to rocks.

Crustaceans (crabs, lobsters, and shrimp) have segmented shells and jointed legs with an external skeleton. Most are saltwater creatures, with crayfish being the freshwater exception.

Cephalopods (cuttlefish, squid, and octopus) have thin internal shells but no outer protection. They have tentacles, attached at the head, which propel them through the water.

Shellfish have been on humankind's menu for centuries and have long been a great source of dietary nutrition. In today's market, shellfish can be an economical source of protein (mussels or periwinkles), as well as a luxury food choice (lobster and scallops). The demand from restaurants, hotels, and home cooks is so great that many types of shellfish are now aqua-farmed to meet it. Shellfish is brought to our shores from all over the world, though shrimp mainly comes from Asian waters or the Gulf of Mexico, while lobster may come from a specific area, such as Maine.

Nutrition

Shellfish are high in protein, iron, and B vitamins, but are relatively low in fat and calories. Most shellfish can be eaten raw, as in raw oysters or sushi, or turned into a wide array of delicious cooked preparations by a talented chef.

Delicate fare

Shellfish is very delicate and only needs the shortest of cooking times, otherwise it will become tough and chewy, so learning to prepare and cook shellfish perfectly, like any other section in the kitchen, takes practice and time.

Fresh or frozen

You can buy shellfish either fresh or frozen. If you are choosing fresh shellfish, look carefully for any signs of movement. Crabs and lobsters should be moving around and mussels, clams, and oysters should be tightly closed, or they should close when you touch them. As they age their shells will begin to open. If they don't snap shut when you touch them, you must discard them since they are dead. All shellfish should have a sweet, sea-like aroma to them.

Purchasing safety points

Just like fish, shellfish decay rapidly because of bacterial action. Shellfish, particularly mollusks, can carry parasites if they have been harvested from contaminated waters, and if they are eaten raw they can transmit gastrointestinal illness. This means that shellfish must only be taken from approved waters. By law each container of shellfish must be tagged, tracking its origins, and food service operations, including restaurants, must keep these tags for 90 days after receiving each consignment.

With the exception of shrimp, which is never alive when brought to the market place, crustaceans should be alive and vigorous when you touch them. Buy only the freshest you can find, from a reputable dealer, since the longer they are in captivity, even live ones lose muscle tissue. For this reason you should purchase them as quickly as possible after they have been caught, and quickly serve them to your customer, to give the best possible freshness and flavor.

76 Workout: Removing meat from crayfish

Crayfish (also known as crawfish) are harvested in freshwater rivers and ponds and can be purchased live or frozen. The tail meat is tender and juicy and the head adds richness to stocks and sauces.

1 Twist the tail from the head and remove two of the uppermost shell sections from the tail so that you expose the flesh.

2 To loosen the meat squeeze the tail with your fingers or snip it with a pair of kitchen scissors.

3 Gently pull the tail meat out in one piece. Then remove the intestinal vein from the tail.

77 Workout: Preparing a cooked lobster

Lobster is one of the most popular and extravagant shellfish eaten anywhere. It can be poached, steamed, baked, or broiled and served hot or cold with melted butter or in hollandaise sauce. When purchased live look for plenty of activity and a well curled-up tail. It should feel heavy for its size. Freezing a live lobster for 15–20 minutes before boiling will immobilize it. Frozen lobster should be bright red and smell fresh. There are two main kinds; those with claws (true or American) and those without (spiny or rock lobsters).

1 Cut the tail in two lengthwise, and cut through the head. Remove and discard the stomach sac from both sides.

2 Remove the intestinal vein and meat, and the tail meat, and set aside.

3 Using your chef's knife, crack open the claws and remove the meat in one piece. Use a rolling pin to roll out the meat from the legs.

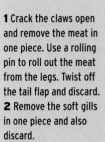

78 Workout: Preparing crab

Boil the crab in salted water for 12–15 minutes, depending on weight and size. Remove and allow the crab to cool. Remove the legs and craws from the body.

1 Crack the claws open and remove the meat in one piece. Use a rolling pin to roll out the meat from the legs. Twist off the tail flap and discard.
2 Remove the soft gills in one piece and also discard.
3 Carefully remove the rest of the brown meat from the shell. You should be left with both white and brown meat.

79 Workout: Preparing a live lobster

There are two ways to cook fresh lobster. If you want to keep it whole, then you really need to boil it. Otherwise you should prepare it as shown in this sequence. Pick up the lobster by holding it just behind the head. If it is very fresh it will arch its back and spread its claws. The claws should be bound with elastic bands, so don't worry about being pinched.

1 Place the live lobster on the chopping board. If it is moving around, this shows that it is fresh and healthy.

2 Take your chef's knife and place it on the natural cross mark on the head. With one swift movement insert the knife.

3 Move the tip of the knife through the head so that it has completely cut through to the chopping board beneath.

4 Turn the lobster 90 degrees and insert the tip of the knife through the tail shell. Cut all the way through.

5 Take one half and carefully remove the stomach sac just behind the eyes and discard. Do the same with the other half.

6 Using a small knife, such as a paring knife, carefully remove the intestinal tract from both sides of the tail meat.

7 Crack open the claws with the back of your chef's knife to ensure even cooking and make it easy to pull out the meat.

Mollusk freshness

Bivalve mollusks, such as mussels, clams, oysters, and scallops, have two shells and live in salt water. Univalves such as winkles, snails, abalone, and conch live in one shell and can be either freshwater, saltwater, or land inhabitants. All mollusks, just like crustaceans and fish, must be extremely fresh in order to be fit for human consumption. Shells should be tightly closed and free of cracks or breaks. Bivalve mollusks may gape slightly, but will close if gently tapped on the shell. If they do not, discard them immediately because they are dead and should not be served. Clams should feel heavy and full when you hold them.

Oysters are more likely to carry bacterial contamination in the summer months. Because of this they carry an age-old safety warning–it's best to eat them only when there is an "R" in the month. The other rule that you must always follow is to to buy oysters only if they bear a harvested tag to identify their origin. Oysters should always be tightly closed.

Oyster safety
A closed shell, or shell that closes when touched, is a sign that the oyster is healthy and fine for eating. Live, or shucked, oysters should have a mild, sweet smell.

Mollusk storage

To store mollusks use the same guidelines as for storing fish (see page 56), but never store them live in plastic bags or ice them down. Keep them in the original box or net bag that they were shipped in and place them on a tray over ice. Cooking and serving methods for mollusks include raw, steamed, boiled, poached, baked, and sautéed.

(see page 56)

Surimi

"Surimi" is a Japanese word meaning "formed fish" and is normally made from pollock or whiting that has been boned, rinsed, and ground into a paste. Flavoring ingredients, such as crab and lobster, are added to the paste, which is then shaped, colored, and cooked. Usually surimi is labeled "imitation crabmeat" or "lobster meat" and it can be used in salads, stews, or soups as an inexpensive alternative to shellfish.

80 Workout: Opening oysters

The best knife to use to open an oyster is an oyster knife, which is made to open shells without damaging the succulent meat. Scrub the oyster shells before you open them. If you are serving them in the half shell, the bottom shell (the deeper of the two) needs to be intact and the oyster undamaged.

1 Wrap your holding hand in a clean dishcloth, making sure none of it is exposed. Grip the oyster in this hand and place the tip of your knife in the point, or hinged end, of the oyster.

2 Be careful, as you may need to use a bit of force. Dig the knife between the two shells at the point and twist to break the hinge.

3 Once the hinge is broken, move your knife gently around the edge of the shell, being careful not to damage the oyster.

4 Continue to slide your knife around the curve of the shell, taking your time. You can now remove the dishcloth and hold the shell in your fingers.

5 Gently remove the top shell with your fingers, carefully releasing the gills with your knife. Remove the lid completely.

6 Being careful not to pierce the oyster or lose any of the natural juices, use your knife to loosen the oyster from the base.

7 Once you have cut through the lower end of the muscle from the bottom shell, the oyster is free.

8 Remove any particles of shell from the oyster before serving.

81 Workout: Preparing squid

Wash and dry the squid, then place it on your chopping board. Start by pulling the head from the main body. This will remove the intestines and the ink sac with one tug. The ink sac looks like a pearly white pouch—this is normally discarded along with the head and intestines.

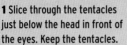

1 Slice through the tentacles just below the head in front of the eyes. Keep the tentacles.

2 Gently pull out the quill from the body sac and discard.

3 Pull away the skin and wash the inside. Now cut the squid into rings or leave it whole.

82 Workout: Preparing scallops

Scallops are collected year-round from shallow and deep water around the world. In Europe both the white meat and the orange crescent coral are eaten, while in the United States only the abductor muscle (the white meat that opens and closes the two shells) is eaten.

1 Place the scallop flat side down, one hand on top to stop movement. Insert the knife tip between the two shells.

2 Start to wiggle your knife while you move it along the edge of the shell. Be sure to take your time.

3 The shell will start to open. Turn your knife 90 degrees, then scrape the bottom shell to cut and release the scallop.

4 The shell will come apart easily now and the contents will be held in the curved part of the shell.

5 Carefully remove everything from the curved shell. To make this task easy, try using a dessertspoon.

6 Discard the gills and black stomach sac. The coral can be eaten if the scallops are fresh.

7 Pull away the membrane and the small, thick muscle that might still be attached to the scallop.

8 The scallop should be free of any membrane. Clean and dried, it is now ready to use.

Cephalopod freshness

Squid, octopus, and cuttlefish all come under the category of cephalopods. They can be purchased fresh or frozen. The ink sacs can be used in other cooking preparations, such as stews or rice dishes like the Spanish "paella." Squid and cuttlefish generally need to be cleaned before cooking, while octopus is usually sold cleaned and most often frozen. As with all shellfish, buy from a reputable dealer and as close to the time of use as possible.

Cephalopod storage

To store cephalopods use the same guidelines as when you are storing fish (see page 56). Cooking methods to choose from include: quickly on a grill; under a broiler; or poached or sautéed (squid and cuttlefish). Octopus needs to be precooked in simmering, salted water, and seasoned with a bouquet garni for one hour, depending on its size and age. Then it can be grilled, sautéed, or stewed.

Serving raw seafood

The coastal cuisines of Japan, the Mediterranean, and South America have served raw shellfish for hundreds of years. Clams and oysters served on the half shell have been offered in traditional high-end restaurants and hotels for decades and are commonplace today in seafood restaurants across all continents. With the explosion of Asian cuisine, more chefs are exploring lighter preparations using raw seafood. Raw shellfish is as much about texture as it is about flavor, so serving crisp accompaniments such as raw vegetables adds contrast, and using zesty flavors such as lemon and lime, fresh herbs, and flavored oils will complement the raw flavor.

Warning

Remember: raw fish or shellfish are potentially hazardous foods and sourcing the freshest products from licensed suppliers is essential. Also, before you add it to your menu, check with the local health department about regulations concerning serving raw food.

Scallops
Scallops are nearly always sold shucked. If available in the shell on the day of their catch, freshness and flavor will be worth the time and effort to remove them from their shells.

Seasonings, stuffings, & coatings

Bringing out the best flavor in your food is a skill you develop through concentration, practice, and a basic understanding of seasonings, stuffings, and coatings.

The finishing touches afforded by seasonings are all part of the chef's fabrication skills-base, which anyone entering the catering industry needs to master. Salt and pepper are a chef's fundamental seasoning, but blends of herbs, spices, and other aromatics can create a particular flavor profile. Stuffings are another way of introducing seasoning to the food—they add moisture and texture to a dish, while breading gives a delicious crisp finish.

Salt and pepper

Learning to season at the right time when you are preparing food will give your finished dish the fullest possible flavor. Salt and pepper are fundamental to bringing out the natural flavor of the meat, poultry, fish, or any other dish. Applying salt and pepper in the early stages of preparing food brings out its inherent flavor, but adding it at the end of the cooking process may cause the dish to be too highly seasoned. This is why it is best to taste as you cook; then you will know when to season properly and sparingly, and be able to judge when you have achieved the desired result. Using your fingertips is the best way of applying salt and pepper, or any other seasoning, since you can control the amount you use and apply an even coating.

Using aromatics

While salt and pepper are seasoning fundamentals, adding various spices, herbs, and other aromatics can give you, as the chef, certain flavor profiles. Just like salt and pepper, herbs and spices need to be applied directly to raw meats, poultry, or fish at the beginning of the cooking stage, so that you can intensify the true flavor of the product.

To deepen the flavor of spices, first toast them, cool, and grind them. Then evenly rub the blend into the product and place it in the refrigerator. This allows the flavors to be absorbed properly.

You can also add spice blends to vegetables. As they cook, the flavor of the spices is released and infused into the dish more effectively as it simmers, especially if the dish happens to be a stew or a braise. Fresh herbs blended with bread crumbs, minced garlic, and grated cheese can also be used as a dry rub or made into a paste and added as a coating for meats, poultry, and fish preparations.

Stuffings

Stuffings add flavor, texture, and moisture and are usually made by combining breadcrumbs and sautéed vegetables. These need to be cooled to 40°F (4°C) before you mix them with chopped herbs, fruit, and spices. You can add fresh stock if you want to add moisture to the dish and also cooked sausage, seafood, or mushrooms to contribute extra flavor and texture, depending on what you are trying to achieve.

You will need to chill the finished stuffing before you use it, and during the final cooking stage it is very important that it reaches the minimum safe temperature for the food into which it is being stuffed.

For this reason, whole turkeys are very rarely stuffed in professional kitchens these days, because of the risk of the meat being overcooked before the stuffing can be cooked all the way through. If stuffing is served, this means that it is usually cooked separately from the turkey and brought to the table alongside it, on the plate, as an accompaniment. However, there is no problem with using stuffing inside smaller food items, including poultry, and still reaching the correct serving temperature.

Basic marinades
Marinades usually contain oils to protect the food from intense heat during cooking; this also adds moisture and flavor. Wine, vinegar, fruit juice, or yogurt are used as an acid on food to help change its texture. You can also use fresh or dried herbs, spices, and vegetables.

Marinades can be dry or wet; the length of time the food is marinated depends on its texture. Delicate fish may only take 10–15 minutes, but a leg of lamb may take hours, or even days, to absorb the flavor. Marinades can be used as a dipping sauce or sometimes as part of the cooking sauce. If raw food has been in the marinade, then you need to boil it to kill any harmful bacteria before you use it. If you are using a wet marinade, make sure that the whole product is submerged to achieve even consistency. Also, if you are grilling or roasting, remove most of the marinade before you start cooking as marinades contain herbs or other aromatics, which can easily burn.

83 Workout: Making breadcrumbs

1 Cube bread that is two to four days old and place it in a food processor. With the lid on, process until you have a fine crumb consistency.

2 To get the best results, after the bread has been processed pass the crumbs through a fine sieve. This will result in a very fine, even grain. You can now add more flavors, such as chopped herbs or spices.

84 Workout: Breading a chicken breast

Breaded foods are generally cooked by either pan-frying or deep-frying. The coating of bread crumbs makes a solid seal around the product, preventing the fat from coming into direct contact with the food. Otherwise it will be very greasy.

1 Pat the chicken breast dry, then dredge it through seasoned flour and shake off the excess.

2 Dip the floured chicken breast into the egg wash (a mixture of whole eggs and milk, blended).

3 Coat the food with the breadcrumb mixture and shake off excess crumbs.

4 Place the finished product on a lined sheet pan. Put it in the refrigerator for at least 30 minutes prior to cooking. This will help the breadcrumbs to adhere to the food.

1

2

3

4

Bread coating

Bread coatings have long been used by chefs to give fried foods protection from the heat of the oil and to create a delicious crisp crust at the same time. Coating with seasoned flour, egg wash, and breadcrumbs is considered the best and most efficient way of coating food to obtain a consistent product.

You can use breadcrumbs that are either fresh or stale, made from corn bread, whole wheat bread, white bread, French stick, or Italian bread. Other options you might consider include seeds, nuts, coconut, cornflakes, grated cheese, garlic paste, or chopped herbs. You can either mix these with the breadcrumbs or use them as a crumb mix on their own.

It's a good idea to use one hand only when you coat items in breadcrumbs, because this leaves you the other, clean, hand available to move equipment or trays around. After using the breading ingredients, discard the trays immediately. Do not be tempted to keep them or reuse them, since this may cause cross-contamination and food poisoning.

85 Workout: Making a dry rub

To make a dry rub, blend fresh or dried herbs and spices together. Use either a mortar and pestle or do it in a food processor. Then apply the rub to the outside of the food product.

86 Workout: Making a herb stuffing for meat or poultry

Bread stuffings are generally flavored with aromatic vegetables, such as onions, garlic, or mushrooms, with the addition of freshly chopped herbs or spices, which are then moistened with wine, stock, or eggs. These are all common ingredients found in any kitchen and they have a dramatic effect on the flavor of the finished product.

1 Take a frying pan and add oil, chopped shallots, garlic, or onions. Cook without coloring for about three to four minutes.

2 Add a splash of white wine or stock and reduce to add flavor and moisture.

3 Add any freshly chopped herbs such as sage, chives, and thyme.

4 Stir in the bread crumbs and mix, taste, and season. Add more stock if needed.

Dry-cooking techniques

Grilling, broiling, roasting, and baking are all methods of cooking that require either direct application of heat or indirect heat, but the result is the same, giving a highly flavored exterior and a moist interior to the product. Sautéeing and pan-frying rely on a certain amount of fat or oil in which to cook the product.

Food suitability
A salmon steak is the perfect choice for the dry-cooking technique.

If you are using smaller-portioned pieces of meat, poultry, or fish, you will find that grilling, broiling, sautéeing, and pan-frying work best. Roasting and baking are usually more appropriate for larger cuts of meat, whole birds, and dressed fish, as they require a longer cooking time.

Grilling and broiling

When food is placed directly onto the grill bars for cooking and the heat comes from beneath, this is known as "grilling," whereas when the heat source comes from above, this is known as "broiling." Usually the food has been brushed with oil or butter, placed on a tray, and positioned under the broiler.

Tender portions of food, such as cuts from the loin, rib, or top round areas from beef, veal, pork, or lamb, poultry, or cuts of fish from salmon and tuna work well grilled or broiled. Less tender cuts of meat can also be used, but you should trim them of their fat and sinew, and cut them into equal sizes. They may need lightly pounding with a mallet to achieve the same thickness. All food needs to be seasoned, lightly oiled, or marinated before being grilled or broiled.

Roasting and baking

Whether roasting or baking, you are using indirect heat to give the food a crispy exterior and a moist interior. As the food's outer layers heat, natural juices turn to steam and cook the food. Always make sure that oven temperature is correct before you start roasting to achieve the best results. Tender cuts from the rib, loin, and leg give best results from beef, veal, pork, and lamb, and whole poultry or game and dressed fish produce great results.

Season well before you place the meat in the oven. Use aromatic vegetables, herbs, spices, or apply a dry rub or slip them under the skin of the food item. You can stuff large joints, whole poultry, chicken breasts, or pork chops before roasting. It is usual to sear large items at a high temperature of 425°F–450°F (218°C–232°C) before turning the heat down to 350°F–375°F (177°–191°C) to give an even-finished cooking.

Sautéeing

"Sautéeing" means to cook food rapidly, in a small amount of fat or oil, over a high heat, and has many similarities to stir-frying. Foods are generally cut into even sizes and cooked in a sequence. Those that require the longest cooking times are cooked first and those that cook

---

87 Workout: Grilling steaks

Pre-heat and clean the grill and have all your *mise en place* ready. Season the steaks, lightly brush the grill bars with oil, and place the steaks on the grill. To achieve grill marks, rotate the steaks through 90 degrees after the first grill marks appear. Turn the steaks over and finish cooking to the required doneness, using Workout 54, page 47, as a guide as required.

---

88 Workout: Carving a roast chicken

Roasting, like baking, is a straightforward cooking technique. Place the meat, poultry, or game on a rack or bed of mirepoix. Cook in a preheated oven temperature, ranging between 325°F–425°F (163°C–218°C) until tender. Roast meats such as chicken need to rest before carving, to allow the meat fibers to relax.

1 Place the chicken on the chopping board and cut through the skin between the leg and breast. Remove the leg.

2 Cut through the breast between the two halves, remove the whole side, then carefully separate the wing from the breast.

3 Repeat on the other side, then cut through the drumstick and thigh, giving you two each of wings, breasts, drumsticks, and thighs.

quickest are added last. The sauce is also made in the same pan, to capture the flavor of the dish as juices from the meat escape into the pan.

Choose cuts from the rib, loin, or leg of beef, veal, lamb, and pork. Poultry and game give good results, as do firm-textured fish such as salmon or monkfish. Shellfish out of the shell also sautée well. You will need a set of tongs to turn foods and remove them from the pan. The menu terms seared/pan-seared, charred, pan-charred, or pan-broiled are all encompassed by "sauté."

Pan-frying

Pan-frying uses more fat or oil to cook the food item than sautéeing. Usually the oil comes halfway to two-thirds up the side of the food being pan-fried; also the heat is not as intense. Pan-fried foods are normally coated in flour, batter, or breading. In pan-frying the heat of the oil seals the food's coated surface, locking in the juices. This means that none of the juices are released into the pan, like sautéeing, so pan sauces are normally made separately.

Naturally tender cuts are used to pan-fry such meats as rib or loin meat, poultry breasts, and lean cuts of fish such as sole or plaice. You need to heat the pan enough to form a nice crust on the outside of the food when you place it in the fat. Then you need to lower the temperature to finish the cooking. It's a good idea to keep paper towels on hand to blot surface fat.

Deep-frying

Deep-frying, like pan-frying, gives a crisp, browned exterior and moist, flavorful interior, but unlike sauté or pan-frying the food is submerged in hot oil. The food is coated with breadcrumbs, batter, or a simpler flour mixture.

89 **Workout:** Sautéeing a chicken breast

Successful sautéeing comes from using a high heat and a minimal amount of fat in the pan to quickly cook the product.

1 Heat the pan over medium-high heat. Add the fat and heat until near smoking point. Add the chicken breast side down first.
2 Cook until the chicken breast has reached the desired color/browning. Turn over and brown on the other side. Cook all the way through.

The food is cooked rapidly and evenly if all the food items are the same size and thickness. Use tender cuts of fish, seafood, chicken, or vegetables. Some vegetables, such as cauliflower or broccoli, may have to be precooked before being deep-fried.

Electric or gas deep-fryers are typically used in professional kitchens. These are safer than using a large pan of oil on the stove. The temperature for frying food is usually between 325°F–375°F (163°C–191°C). The oil will drop in temperature when you add the food, so only add one or two items at a time, otherwise it will take longer to return to the correct temperature. Prepare a tray lined with paper towels to blot the fat from the food.

90 **Workout:** Making a pan sauce

Pan sauces normally accompany many sautéed foods. These sauces often incorporate the liquid produced by deglazing the pan after removing the cooked product. "Deglazing" means removing the cooked food particles that are stuck to the bottom of the pan with a liquid such as stock or wine. The deglazed liquid is then used as the base of the pan sauce to contribute color and flavor.

1 After you have removed the cooked food, pour off excess fat. Add aromatics and wine.

2 The wine will release any browned drippings that have caramelized on the bottom of the pan.

3 Reduce the wine until nearly dry, then add the stock along with cream, if you are using it.

4 The sauce may need thickening with a little corn starch mixed with water and brought to a boil to thicken.

5 If you are not using a thickening agent, reduce until you have the desired consistency. Then taste and finish with chopped fresh herbs.

Moist-cooking techniques

Steaming and submersion are moist-cooking techniques, which also cover *en papillote*, shallow-poaching, deep-poaching, and simmering as methods of covering the product in liquid or water vapor as the cooking medium. Braising and stewing have always been considered "peasant" cooking methods, since less-expensive main ingredients, such as tough cuts of meat, have traditionally been used.

As an aspiring chef you might want to experiment by altering the ingredients for braising and stewing and try using poultry, fish, shellfish, or vegetables, making dishes lighter in flavor and color and more appropriate for today's health-conscious customer.

Steaming
Steaming is a method of cooking in which the food is totally surrounded by water vapor in an enclosed cooking vessel. Ideal for fish or poultry, steaming retains more intrinsic flavor. Food generally does not lose size or volume and the finished dish is usually plump, moist, and tender. Different liquids can be used for the steaming, such as water, broth, stock, or a court bouillon, wine, or even beer. These will all impart flavor to the food items being cooked. Aromatics such as herbs or spices, garlic, ginger, shallots, mushrooms, or even a bed of vegetables can contribute flavor or be used as part of the dish.

En papillote
En papillote is another steaming technique, however this time you wrap the main food item and accompanying ingredients in a bag made of parchment paper and cook it in the oven until the paper has expanded and is brown in color. It can be difficult to gauge whether the food is cooked or not, because you can't open the bag to see if it is done—steam needed for cooking the item would be released. As when you are steaming, you should choose tender foods such as fish, seafood, or poultry and cut them to even-sized portions. Usually finely cut vegetables are added, which might need precooking, plus herbs and spices, along with a splash of wine to act as the vapor when heated.

Shallow-poaching
Shallow-poached foods are cooked by a combination of steaming and simmering as the food is partially submerged in liquid, which is normally a fresh stock, or rich broth with the addition of vinegar or wine to act as an acid. Aromatic flavors can be added, such as finely chopped shallots, celery, and fresh herbs. The cooking liquid is usually reduced and turned into an accompanying sauce. Trimmed fish, chicken breasts, and shellfish all poach well. You can use a sauté pan or shallow saucepan for poaching and make a lid out of buttered parchment paper so that it fits loosely and traps enough steam

91 **Workout:** Cooking *en papillote*

To cook *en papillote*, cut a piece of parchment into a heart-shaped piece, large enough to contain the portion of fish and vegetables. Brush the paper with melted butter, place it on the fish and the finely chopped vegetables, and add a small quantity of wine. Fold over and crimp the edges of the paper to seal them together, then bake in the oven until cooked.

to cook the unexposed part of the food. Tongs and a spatula will come in handy to lift out the cooked items; also you may require a strainer to finish off the sauce.

Deep-poaching and simmering
Deep-poaching and simmering are both very similar in that the food is completely submerged in liquid such as a rich stock, broth, or court bouillon. Deep-poaching is done at a slightly lower temperature than simmering and is appropriate for tender cuts of meat, poultry, and fish, whereas simmering is used for tougher cuts and cooks at a slightly higher temperature. You can deep-poach or simmer whole items, including dressed fish, whole poultry, or a large piece of meat. You really need a large pot or poaching pan to successfully deep-poach or simmer. Leave the lid off since it may cause the liquid to become hotter than you want it. Deep-poaching should be at a temperature of 160°F–180°F (71°C–82°C), while simmering should be 185°F–205°F (85°C–95°C). Keep a thermometer handy to maintain the liquid at the correct temperature.

Braising
Braising is usually for tough, whole cuts of meat that have been trussed to keep an even size and shape. Season the meat well and sear it in a hot pan to add color, then place it on a bed of vegetables in a braising pot. Now add hot stock or a combination of stock and sauce to a

The importance of seasoning
Moist-cooking techniques are not complete until the food has been tasted, its flavor evaluated, and seasoning adjusted to bring out the best possible flavor in the foods.

third or halfway up the piece of meat. You then place a lid on the pot and put it into an oven to slowly simmer until cooked and tender all the way through. As the moisture gently penetrates the meat it breaks down the connective tissues, making them soft and tender. Also the flavor released from the meat into the sauce makes it flavorsome. Choose a large, heavy braising pan, or rondeau, with a lid for slow, even cooking. A kitchen fork to check for doneness and to remove the meat from the pan, plus a carving knife, will come in handy.

Stewing

Stewing is very similar to braising, only you use tough cuts of meat that have been cut into smaller sizes and you use more liquid. Stews are normally considered a one-pot meal because you have the meat, poultry, or seafood as the main food ingredient and vegetables and a rich-flavored sauce all served together out of one pot.

Trim the food of excess fat, gristle, and sinew, cut into even-sized cubes, season with either salt and pepper or a dry rub or marinade. Choose a heavy braising pan, or rondeau, heat and sear the cubed food, add a rich stock, and bring to a simmer. Add peeled, uniform-sized vegetables as the cooking process continues. Test with a fork to see if the meat is tender or remove a small portion to taste. You can finish the sauce with cream, fresh herbs, or a thickening agent such as a *beurre manié* or a liaison of eggs and cream.

92 Workout: Braising

Sear the meat in hot oil in a large pan. Then remove the meat, add the mirepoix of vegetables, deglaze with wine, and add stock two-thirds up the side of the meat. Then bring to a simmer, return the food, covered, to the oven. When fork-tender the dish is done. Strain the liquid and thicken or adjust seasoning and serve with the meat.

Stews of the world

Whatever country you live in or travel to, you will come across a traditional stew. Most are peasant dishes that have been in existence for centuries. Learn their history and enjoy their flavors.

Name	Main ingredients	Country of origin
Chili con carne	ground/diced beef or lamb, beans	Chile and Mexico
England boil	corned beef brisket	United States
Fricassee	white meat chicken or game	France
Goulash	beef	Hungary
Irish lamb stew	boneless lamb shoulder/shank	Ireland
Lamb tagine	meat, chicken, fish, vegetables	North Africa

93 Workout: Cubing meat for stews

Stewing uses moist heat to tenderize meat: you can use many of the same meats as for braising. For stewing, the meat should be trimmed of excess fat and connective tissue and cut into 1–2 in (2.5–5 cm) cubes, unlike braised meat cubes, which are trimmed and left whole.

1 Remove the bone from the meat, if necessary, and then start to remove any sinew or excess fat.

2 Taking your time, using either a boning knife or chef's knife, continue to trim off excess sinew.

3 Leave any tough sinew or silver skin on the board as you carefully remove the lean meat.

4 Trim any further fat away. Remember that fat gives flavor, so don't remove too much.

5 Cut the meat into evenly sized pieces of about 1–2 in (2.5–5 cm).

4

Vegetables, fruits, grains, & dried goods

The human race has been cultivating vegetables and fruits since before the rise of civilization, but for too long vegetables and fruits have been overcooked and underrated; second-class citizens to the proteins on the plate. However, they are enjoying a welcome return today, as chefs follow the seasons and take advantage of the abundance of fresh produce available at local farmers' markets throughout the year. This section will help you learn how to pick the best vegetables and fruits at their peak flavor and highest nutritional value. It will help you find out what's in season and what to look for in terms of quality and ripeness; learn how to wash, prepare, and store produce correctly to retain natural properties.

Grains are a nutritional staple in most parts of the world and cover everything from wheat, corn, cornmeal, grits, rice, couscous, barley, oats, and quinoa to flours that are used to make bread, cakes, pasta, and noodles. Learn about all the different grains and their uses in the kitchen and the many different varieties of rice and how to cook it. Learn how to make fresh pasta, which is a simple mixture of wheat flour and liquid, and see how pasta has traveled beyond its original Italian borders to become one of the most popular foods on the planet.

Seasonality

"Seasonality" of food refers to the times of year when a given type of food is at its peak, either in terms of harvest or its flavor.

Seasonality is very important to chefs. If the food is not in season it won't be of the best quality. Buying from local farmers means that the product does not have to travel far, indicating that it is fresher and tastier.

Chefs are eager to support local farmers in every way they can, and buying locally helps the farmer and also puts money back into the community. Local farmers select, grow, and harvest crops to ensure peak qualities of freshness, nutrition, and taste. Eating locally also means eating seasonally, a practice that is in tune with nature.

The food's peak time, in terms of harvest, usually coincides with when its flavor is at its best. There are some exceptions, an example being sweet potatoes, which are best eaten a while after harvest. Eating seasonally has been practiced since ancient times, since people ate what nature produced, according to the seasons.

Pluses of seasonal produce

In almost every circumstance, seasonal produce is at its peak in terms of flavor, nutrition, and price. Seasonality also helps local industry and gives customers the chance to taste locally grown products. Seasonal produce has not been forced to bear fruit or produce leaves or flowers through the use of hothouses or other means of making plants produce food. It tastes the way it should, riper and more full-flavored.

Cooking with seasonal produce works well in so many ways and most chefs favor this approach. A winter braise served with carrots, swedes, and turnips makes perfect sense, as this is the time of year when these vegetables are at their very best. A berry pudding on a hot summer's day, made from berries in season, served with cream, makes for a stunning dessert that your customers will love.

Produce comes into season at roughly the same time each year, with regional variations. This means that there may be a glut on the market and prices may be competitive. Consider the difference in the price of a hothouse tomato from Australia in January to that of a tomato from your local farmers' market in summer, and also compare the taste. Seasonal produce is cheaper, helping local farmers and food businesses with food costs. And it also makes better environmental sense when you take into account the carbon footprint of produce that has traveled halfway around the globe.

Harvesting strawberries
Strawberries are in season late spring to early summer. Look for bright-colored berries.

What's available and when

Most produce is available all year round, but it is at its best condition and best price in the season in which it is harvested. Because the country is so large, seasonality also depends on the specific state and region. This is a general list of what is available during which season.

Spring
Fruits and vegetables: apricots, pineapple, strawberries, mangoes, peas (sugarsnap and snow) and more delicate cabbages, mustard greens, baby lettuce, baby spinach, and watercress. Also in season are artichoke, asparagus, avocado, new potatoes, and rhubarb.

Seafood: clams, cockles, red sea beam, sardines, skipjack tuna.
Game: grouse and hare.

Summer
Fruits and vegetables: some berries (blackberries, blueberries, raspberries) and stone fruit (nectarines, peaches, and plums) as well as melons, beets, corn, cucumber, eggplant, green beans, tomatoes, and zucchini.

Seafood: soft-shell crab, crayfish, sea bass, sea trout, clams, rainbow trout, John Dory.

Fall
Fruits and vegetables: apples, grapes, figs, pears, pomegranates, many cultivars of wild cabbage (broccoli, Brussels sprouts, cauliflower, collards, endives, and kale). Root vegetables (garlic, ginger, parsnips, turnips, and yams) and winter squash (acorn squash, butternut squash, and pumpkins) are also in season.

Corn is in season and peas, seasonal in spring, are also seasonal in late fall.
Seafood: mackerel, salmon, oysters.
Game: deer, elk, moose.

Winter
Fruits and vegetables: include citrus (clementines, grapefruit, oranges, and lemons) and pomegranates. Winter vegetables include hardier cabbages (kale, leeks, radicchio, and Brussels sprouts). Also seasonal in winter are some root vegetables (rutabaga,

turnips, and radishes) as well as winter squash.
Game: duck and goose.
Seafood: sea bass, scallops, Pacific yellowtail tuna, Pacific cod, monkfish, halibut, lobster, mussels, stone crab.

94 Workout: Ask questions

When you go to the farmers' market, ask the local farmer as many questions as you can: how the vegetables and fruits are grown, how the chickens are looked after to get the best supply of eggs, and how the cattle or sheep are reared to get the best-quality meat.

Look at the other sections in this book on the quality points of produce, meat, and fish. This will make it easier to have a good conversation with the farmer. If you are familiar with the basics on what to look for in products, you stand a better chance of finding out useful information.

95 Workout: Taste-test heirloom tomatoes

Check out your local farmers' market and do a taste-test. Try some heirloom tomatoes from one of the stalls and compare the taste with regular tomatoes from your local store. You could also do a blind taste test with your family or friends and see what their reactions are. First off, can they tell the difference? Normal supermarket tomatoes, especially out of season, taste bland, so if your tasters have never tasted a locally grown tomato in season they are in for a real treat. Try the test with other vegetables and experience the difference. Buying produce with great flavor means that you need very little preparation; you are tasting the natural flavor as opposed to covering it with a heavy sauce or dressing.

96 Workout: Preparing artichokes

Artichokes are the immature flower of a thistle plant, originating in Italy and Spain. You can steam, simmer, or microwave whole artichokes and serve them with lemon juice, garlic butter, or hollandaise sauce. You can also trim them down to just the heart and serve them in salads or purées, or fill them with peas and serve as a side. As soon as you have prepared them rub them with lemon juice, as they discolor quickly.

1 Hold the artichoke head in one hand. Trim off the woody stem with a serrated knife.

2 Make the base as flat as possible.

3 Remove the tough outer leaves by carving around the edge of the head.

4 Using a paring knife, trim the edges of the artichoke to give a pleasant and even appearance.

5 Cut off the excess leaves. Then use a spoon or your knife to remove the choke from the middle of the artichoke.

74 Fruits

Fruits are the ovaries that surround or contain the seeds of plants, and they can be used throughout the menu, both savory and sweet. Fried fruits can be found in salsa, compotes, sauces, and stuffings.

Fruit history

Scientists have carbon-dated apple seeds back to 6,500 BC and later the Romans used to cultivate apples to make apple juice. Apricot trees were cultivated in England in the 1300s, and they were brought to North America, along with pear trees, as early as the 1600s.

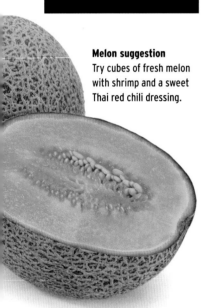

Melon suggestion
Try cubes of fresh melon with shrimp and a sweet Thai red chili dressing.

Fruit in the diet

Fruits have always been a very important part of the human diet and today chefs need to take advantage of the abundance of fresh produce available in local stores and at farmers' markets.

Fruits supply the body with energy through the natural sugars that they contain; they are also good providers of fiber to help with digestion. Many fresh fruits are high in vitamins and minerals and rich in antioxidants called "phytonutrients," which help in fighting heart disease, cancers, and other illnesses.

Fresh fruits

"Fresh" fruits are those that have not been canned, frozen, or dried, and they come in eight categories: citrus fruits, melons, berries, drupes, pomes, grapes, tropical, and exotic.

Citrus fruits have been grown for more than 6,000 years. They are identified by their bright-colored thick rind and bitter pith, which is the skin that holds the bitter-sweet segmented fruit together. Lemons, limes, grapefruits, kumquats, oranges, and tangerines all fall into the category of citrus.

Melons are 90 percent water and can be divided into two groups: sweet and water. They are best served uncooked because of their high water content. Melons are ideal fresh in fruit salads and served with cured meats such as Parma ham. They come in all shapes, sizes, colors, and flavors. To test for ripeness, the blossom end should yield slightly to pressure if you squeeze it. Varieties include cantaloupe, casaba, honeydew, Santa Claus, and watermelon.

Berries, such as blackberries, blueberries, cranberries, raspberries, gooseberries, and strawberries, are all great sources of potassium, fiber, and vitamin C. They grow on bushes and vines and ripen on the vine, so if you buy berries that are plump and juicy, they will deteriorate quickly if you don't store them correctly. Berries are ideal for jams, preserves, and jellies, but are great to eat raw—or you can use them in baked desserts or pastry goods.

Drupes contain a large stone, or pit. This category includes highly perishable fruits such as apricots, cherries, peaches, nectarines, plums, and olives, which are all at their best in the summer months. Delicious to eat fresh or dried, drupes are also used in the production of many brandies and liqueurs.

97 Workout: Coring an apple

Either use an apple corer or quarter the apple with your paring knife. Then lay it flat side down and cut out the core horizontally, taking as little apple flesh away as possible.

98 Workout: How to prepare a mango

Mango is one of the most delicious fruits in the world; fabulous on its own, cut into slices or cubes, or turned into a salsa and served with roasted sea bass. Alternatively it can be made into a soufflé with mango ice cream and served as a wonderful dessert. When you are preparing it bear in mind that it has a rather large stone at its center.

1 Place the mango on your chopping board and position your knife just slightly away from the center. Cut through to the board.

2 Score the mango flesh with your knife from top to bottom, being careful not to cut through the skin.

3 Make incisions across the width of the mango, in a crisscross pattern. Repeat steps 1–3 on the other side of the mango.

4 Now pop the mango by pushing upward through the skin. To make cubes just slice off the mango chunks.

Pomes are grown on trees and contain a central core holding many seeds. The skin is thin and the flesh is firm—the best known are apples and pears. There are hundreds of varieties of apples. Pears are grown worldwide.

Grapes are classified by color: green are referred to as "white" and red are referred to as "black." Table grapes are available all year round and are used in fruit salads or as an accompaniment to fish, cheese, or desserts. Varieties include Champagne, originally used to make wine and raisins, Concord, commonly used for jelly and juice, Emperor, best served in salads, snacks, or in desserts, and Thompson, sweet and crisp, the predominant table variety.

Tropical fruit are available year round and are grown in tropical regions. Because of modern transportation and refrigeration, tropical fruits can be purchased anywhere around the globe. Bananas, plantains, coconuts, dates, kiwis, and mangoes, papayas, passion fruit, and pineapples all come under the heading "tropical."

Exotic fruits are classified as figs, guavas, feijoa, lychee, pomegranates, star fruit, and prickly pears, which are commonly grown in South America, California, Florida, or China.

Buying and storing fruit

Some fresh fruits are shipped washed, cleaned, peeled, and cut up and ready to use. Some fruit is harvested ripe, for example strawberries, while other fruit is harvested unripe, such as bananas. All fruit deteriorates after reaching full ripeness, so it should be stored in a clean, cool environment and used quickly.

Canned, frozen, and dried

Most canned fruit is preserved in water, fruit juice, or syrup. Heating kills harmful bacteria, but has little effect on nutritional value. It can be stored in a cool, dry place; once opened it should be removed from the can and placed in an airtight container in the refrigerator. Damaged cans must be discarded. Today most fruit is individually quick-frozen (IQF). This method is quick and reduces formation of ice crystals. Dried fruits are preserved with an age-old method that can be used on most fruits. When dried, flavor and sweetness is intensified because of lack of water. Store dried fruits in airtight containers, away from moisture and direct sunlight. Before use, soak in hot water or wine, brandy, or rum. Some dried fruits benefit from being simmered.

Pineapple suggestion
Serve grilled pineapple with pork chops or with ice cream for dessert.

---

99 Workout: How to peel an orange

You can easily remove the skin from an orange using these two simple methods, depending on what you are using the orange for. One method removes the skin only, while the second method removes both skin and pith, leaving just the juicy segments.

1 Score the skin around the orange, then between the scoring lines. Remove the quarters of skin.

2 Or, use a serrated knife and follow the natural curve of the orange, taking off the skin and pith.

100 Workout: How to segment an orange

Once you have removed the skin and pith from the orange, take your time in removing one segment at a time to produce the juiciest pieces possible. Use them in salads, or as garnishes for a roast duck main course, or in a fruit salad.

1 Holding the orange in one hand and your knife in the other, cut between the segment lines.

---

101 Workout: How to prepare lemon wedges

Lemon wedges are often served with fish and shellfish: the citrus juice enhances and enlivens the dishes. They are also used as a garnish on many other food presentations, as well as in iced water or in carbonated and alcoholic drinks.

1 Start by cutting the pointed ends of the lemon off. Then, holding the lemon with the claw grip, cut in half lengthwise.

2 Place the lemon flat side down on the board and cut it in half again, to give you quarters.

3 Depending on what size and how many slices you need, you can cut the lemon into eighths.

4 Keeping the lemon wedge on one of the flat sides, cut away the pith to make it easier for your customer to squeeze.

Vegetables

"Vegetable" refers to any herbaceous plant that can be partially or wholly eaten raw or cooked. This includes eating the leaves, stems, roots, tubers, seeds, and flowers. A herbaceous plant usually has very little, if any, woody tissue and contains more starch and less sugar than fruit.

Human beings have been cultivating plant food from their very beginnings. Ancient Egyptians and Sumerians (circa 3000 BC) enjoyed a rich diet of vegetables. Vegetables contain between 65 and 95 percent water, are low in fats, carbohydrates, and protein, but are very high in fiber. Included in the term "vegetable" are all the following plant categories: leafy vegetables, brassicas, shoot vegetables, fruit vegetables, squashes and gourds, bulbs, roots and tubers, pods and seeds, and mushrooms and truffles.

Leafy vegetables

Leafy vegetables include spinach, Swiss chard, endive, sorrel, lettuce, and watercress. Most are strong in flavor, with spicy hints, and they contain a large amount of water. They can be served raw or cooked, though when cooked they will drastically reduce in volume. When purchasing leafy vegetables, look for brightly colored leaves that are crisp in texture, with no brown spots.

Brassicas

The edible parts of brassicas are the flower heads. They include green cabbage, broccoli, cauliflower, boy chow, Brussels spouts, and red cabbage. Brassicas are mostly mild in flavor, quick to grow, inexpensive to buy, readily available, and easy to prepare. Eaten raw or cooked, heads, flowers, and leaves can all be used. When purchasing, look for firm texture, fresh, appealing, crisp, compact leaves, with no brown spots.

Shoot vegetables

Shoot vegetables include artichokes, asparagus, bamboo shoots, fennel, celery, and palm hearts. They are harvested while young and tender, since if they are left too long before being picked they will become tough and fibrous.

Fruit vegetables

Fruit vegetables include avocado, chili peppers, eggplant, tomatoes, and bell peppers. They are classed as fruit because they develop from the ovary of flowering plants and contain one or more seeds. When purchasing, look for smooth, unblemished skins.

Squashes and gourds

Squashes and gourds come from a family of over 750 species, including yellow squash, zucchini, acorn squash, butternut squash, pumpkin, and cucumbers, and they come in all shapes and sizes. Squashes are usually classified as either

102 Workout: Preparing avocados

Avocados are pear-shaped fruits rich in high-fat flesh, which is golden green in color, surrounding a large inedible oval-shaped seed. Avocados come in several varieties: some are smooth and green-skinned, while others are pebbly, almost black in color. Ripe avocados should be soft to touch but not too mushy.

1 Gently cut horizontally through to the stone, then roll the fruit around the knife 360 degrees.

2 Using your hands, twist the avocado halves in opposite directions to separate from the stone.

3 Depending on ripeness, the stone may fall out. If not, use your knife to gently lever the stone out.

4 Cut into quarters, then hold each quarter and carefully peel back the skin.

103 Workout: Preparing kale

Kale is becoming increasingly popular, having been sadly ignored for decades. Full of nutrients, it is a hardy variety of leaf vegetable, which may have a woody stem that needs to be removed with a knife.

1 To remove the woody stem, trim the kale at the base so that the stalks are released.

2 Taking one stalk at a time, cut along the side to separate it from the leaves. Remove, using your fingers. You can then either leave the leaves whole or chop them up.

104 Workout: Peeling and slicing onions

Onions are strong-flavored, aromatic members of the lily family. They are used by almost every culture in the world as a vegetable side or for adding flavor to stocks, soups, sauces, and numerous other dishes.

1 Place the whole onion on the chopping board and cut through the root, giving you two equal halves.
2 Remove the skin from the onion, leaving the root intact. This will help keep the onion together when you slice it.
3 Place the onion half, flat side down, on the chopping board. Using your knuckles as a guide, slice through the onion flesh, giving you even slices.

winter or summer squash. The blossoms are edible and the cavities are full of seeds. When purchasing, look for squashes and gourds that are firm and free of mold and blemishes.

Bulb vegetables

Bulb vegetables include garlic, leeks, onions, and shallots. The onion is one of the most widely used vegetables around the world and it is used in nearly every cuisine. Bulbs should be firm and have a good color to them, having no mold or black spots.

Roots and tubers

Roots are the deep taproots of plants, while tubers are the fat underground stems. The root and tuber family includes carrots (the most popular of the taproots), beetroots, celeriac, jicama, parsnips, potatoes (the most popular tuber), and turnips. Look for roots and tubers that have good color, without blemishes or wrinkles, and are firm in texture.

Pods and seeds

Pods and seeds include peas, bean sprouts, corn, green beans, haricot verts, and okra. Normally just the seeds are eaten, but in some cases the whole pod (okra) is edible. When purchasing pods and seeds, look for good shapes, unblemished skins, and firm texture.

Mushrooms and truffles

Mushroom varieties include white, button, portabello, shiitake, and cromini. Mushrooms are not really a vegetable, because they have no seeds, stems, or flowers, and they are from the fungi family. However, they are prepared just like vegetables. When purchasing mushrooms, look for blemish-free items with no dark spots. If they are dirty, try to brush off the dirt, or just before using gently wash them under cold running water. Do not allow them to soak in water. Pat dry before using.

Truffles come in two varieties: black (Périgord) and white (Piemont) and are found at the bases of oak or beech trees. Truffles are very expensive and are very perishable when purchased fresh, so many food service operators buy them canned, dried, or processed. The Piemont varieties are generally used in sauces, soups, pasta, and rice dishes. Périgord are used in forcemeats such as terrines, pâtés, and as a garnish in certain dishes.

Black truffles
Considered a great delicacy, reflected in their high price, these are often used to flavor pâtés and terrines, and to garnish egg dishes.

Cooking guidelines

Whatever method you choose for cooking vegetables, you will need to follow some general guidelines:

• Promote even cooking and appearance by cutting vegetables carefully into uniform sizes and shapes.

• Cook vegetables for the shortest amount of time possible to retain their texture, color, and nutrients.

• Cook vegetables as close to service time as possible.

• Cook white or red vegetables with a little acid, such as lemon juice, white wine, or vinegar to help retain color.

• If you are preparing an assortment of vegetables, cook them separately before combining.

• You can blanche (partly cook) vegetables and refresh them in ice-cold water, drain, refrigerate, then reheat when you need them.

Storing garlic
Garlic should be stored in a cool, dry, well-ventilated area off the ground. Do not refrigerate unless you have any preprepared left over (place it in an airtight container).

The appeal of vegetables

Vegetables are enjoying a welcome return in popularity among the best chefs around the world, and the increased demand from vegetarians and vegans has put them in the spotlight. Overcooked, overlooked, and underrated in times gone by, vegetables prepared properly add flavor, color, and variety to almost any dish on the menu.

Diners are more knowledgeable and health-conscious than ever before and they demand high-quality, fresh produce prepared and served at its best. Because they are so perishable, vegetables require extra care and attention from the moment they are received to when they are served. Freshness and seasonality are their most appealing qualities, so using vegetables at their seasonal peak has several advantages: prices are at their lowest, selection at its greatest, and the vegetables' color, flavor, texture, and nutritional value are at their peak.

Nutrition

Most vegetables are more than 80 percent water, the remaining 20 percent consisting of carbohydrates and small amounts of protein and

Markets
Farmers' markets are the best places to buy fresh produce in season. You'll get it at its peak.

fat, vitamins and minerals. Vegetables are also relatively low in calories and their structure is fibrous, making their texture crisp and stringy.

Purchasing and storing

Fresh vegetables are at their best when they are in season, and they are sold by weight or count and packed in cases, lugs, bushels, flats, or crates. Certain vegetables, such as onions, carrots, celery, and lettuce, can be purchased cleaned, trimmed, and cut according to your specifications. The price will be higher, but this might be worth it if you are saving time, labor, yield loss, and storage space. Vegetables do not ripen in the same manner as fruits, but they continue to breathe after harvesting, and the faster they breathe, the faster they decay.

Vegetables such as potatoes, onions, shallots, and garlic can be stored at 40°F–60°F (4°C–16°C), ideally in a separate produce refrigerator or stored at room temperature in a dry area with good ventilation. Do not store vegetables in a conventional refrigerator, since this is too cold and it will turn the starches into sugars, changing their texture and flavor. Most other vegetables can be stored at 34°F–40°F (2°C–4°C) with high levels of humidity.

105 Workout: Fanning an avocado

Avocados cut in two make great containers to hold shrimp or crab salad and mashed or puréed make guacamole or other flavorsome dips. Peeled and fanned they make a spectacular presentation to a finished dish or buffet display.

1 Using your chef's knife, cut through the flesh lengthwise in parallel slices, but without cutting all the way through.

2 Pick up the avocado in both hands and gently press down and away to fan out the slices.

3 Return the avocado to the chopping board and carefully press out the slices even more to create the finished fan effect.

106 Workout: How to make a tomato rose

Preparing a tomato rose is a great way to enhance your knife skills and at the same time add impact and color to your plate presentations. After a little practice you'll find that it's surprisingly easy to make.

1 Take a firm tomato and your turning knife and slice across the bottom of the tomato, leaving about a sliver intact for the base.

2 Start to cut with your knife, making a spiral of peel. Keep close to the chopping board so that the weight of the peel does not break.

3 Continue to cut, making sure you are taking the same thickness and width off the tomato, until you have one long peeling.

4 Using both hands, wind up the skin tightly on itself until it reaches the base that it will sit on.

107 Workout: Preparing tomato concasse

Tomato concasse is used to enhance the flavor and finish of sauces and dishes. Start by marking a shallow X in the bottom of the tomato. Then drop it in boiling water for 20 seconds, remove, and place in a container of ice-cold water to stop the cooking process.

1 With your paring knife remove the skin, which should come off easily. Then cut the tomato into quarters.
2 Carefully remove the seeds and the core. Save them to add to stocks for flavor.
3 Now you will have four pieces of tomato resembling leaves. Take your knife and cut them into thin, evenly sized strips.
4 Gather up the strips, then cut them into small dice. You can use these to garnish sauces, soups, and salads.

Preserving vegetables

Preserved vegetables are designed to extend the shelflife of vegetables.

Irradiation uses gamma rays of cobalt-60 or cesium-137 to sterilize vegetables. Radiation kills parasites, insects, and bacteria and slows down the ripening of the food. The flavor and texture are not affected, but the shelflife is extended. Irradiated vegetables should be stored the same way as fresh ones.

Freezing vegetables is a highly effective method of preserving because it severely inhibits microorganisms from growing without destroying many of the plant's nutrients. Some vegetables can be frozen raw while others need to be blanched before freezing so that final cooking time is reduced and color is preserved. Frozen vegetables should be stored at a temperature of 0°F (-18°C).

Canned vegetables are raw vegetables that have been cleaned, portioned, and placed in sealed containers before being subjected to high temperatures for a specific period of time. The heating destroys the microorganisms that can cause spoilage and the sealing retards decomposition. The heat can affect the color and texture of the vegetables. Canned foods stored at room temperature will last almost indefinitely, but once opened the unused contents should be transferred to a storage container with a lid before being labeled, dated, and refrigerated. Cans with bulges should be discarded immediately.

Drying vegetables dramatically affects the flavor, texture, and appearance, and the lack of moisture concentrates the sugars, which greatly adds to the selflife. Not many vegetables are dried, the main ones being beans, peas, peppers, mushrooms, and tomatoes.

80 Grains

Grains are the seeds of edible grasses and they are a nutritional staple in most parts of the world. The category covers everything from wheat, corn, cornmeal, grits, rice, couscous, barley, oats, and quinoa to flours used for making bread, cakes, pasta, and noodles.

Cooking variations
You can cook grains using the pilaf method. Use hot oil or butter to cook aromatic vegetables, adding the rice and coating it in the fat before pouring in a white stock and cooking it in the oven.

Depending on how much the grains have been processed, they are an excellent source of vitamins, minerals, proteins, and fiber. Grains are made up of the bran, endosperm, and the germ. The bran is a good source of fiber and B-vitamins, the endosperm provides protein and carbohydrates, and the germ provides fat.

Identifying grains

Wheat is most commonly used to make flour. The milling process for white flour separates the bran and germ. Wheat germ and wheat bran can be purchased separately. Flour makes bread, cakes, pasta, and noodles.

Corn use dates back thousands of years. Unlike other grains, which have a husk covering each seed, corn has a set of husks covering the entire seed head or ear. It is the only grain that is eaten in its fresh state as "corn on the cob."

Cornmeal comes from corn called "dent," which can be yellow, white, or blue in color. It is often used in breads such as "corn bread" or cooked and served as polenta, or used as a bread coating on fried or deep-fried products.

Grits are white granules made from hominy (flour made from dried corn kernels) that are normally served at breakfast or as a favorite in the southern states of the United States.

Rice is a staple food for over half of the world's population. It is the seed of a semi-aquatic grass. Rice is very versatile and can be served with almost any cuisine, from Indian to Chinese, to traditional French, or as a British classic such as baked rice pudding. It can be served in its own right or as a side dish; its texture adds chewiness to meat, poultry, fish, salads, breads, and puddings.

Rice is divided into three main groups based on the size of the seed: long grain, medium grain, and short grain. Long grain is the most widely used because it is the most versatile. Medium grain has a higher starch content and is best eaten freshly made since it will stick together when cold. Short grain is used for making sushi, risotto, or paella, because it becomes tender and sticky when it is cooked.

All rice is brown in color due to the bran husk covering it, but it can be processed into different forms from brown rice, white rice, converted rice, and instant rice to quick-cooking rice. Some of the nutrients and flavor are lost due to processing. Wild rice comes in three grades: giant, which is considered the best quality, with long, slender grains; fancy, which is medium-sized and the most commonly used; and select, which is short-grained and used in soups and

108 Workout: Molding rice

Rice is so versatile that you can serve it with most things. Instead of placing a pile of it on the plate or in a circle to enclose a curry, why not try molding it into a shape that will add visual appeal to the plate? This is so easy and it adds a professional finish. However, you should remember that risotto should never be molded.

1 Make your rice and while it is still warm fill a timbale mold or cookie cutter ring with the rice, making sure you firmly pack the rice into it. Place the filled mold in the center of the plate, or to one side.

2 Carefully lift off the mold and place or ladle the other food items around the rice. Serve.

109 Workout: Making a risotto

"Risotto" is the traditional name of this classic Italian dish and the cooking method. As you add more stock, you continually stir the rice to bring out the starch, which thickens the stock into a sauce.

1 Warm the stock in one saucepan and heat the oil in another to slowly cook the aromatic ingredients. Add the rice and stir to coat with the oil.

2 Add part of the warm stock and keep stirring until all the liquid has been absorbed.

3 Continue to add the stock in small amounts to the rice and stir until it has all been used and the rice is tender.

4 Finish the risotto with cubes of butter, grated cheese, or crème fraîche.

110 Workout: Cooking couscous

Couscous is very easy to make and you can serve it, just like rice, with most meats, fish, poultry, vegetables, or on its own as a salad. To serve four people start with 6 oz (180 g) couscous, 1 cup (240 ml) chicken stock, 1 tbsp (20 g) melted butter, sea salt, and freshly ground black pepper.

1 Place the couscous in a bowl or tray. Bring the chicken stock to a boil in a saucepan.

2 Ladle the chicken stock over the couscous and stir once with a wooden spoon.

3 Cover the tray tightly with plastic wrap and allow the couscous to rest for 20 minutes while it absorbs the liquid.

 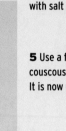

4 Remove the plastic wrap and pour the melted butter over the couscous. Season with salt and pepper.

5 Use a fork to fluff up the couscous, layer by layer. It is now ready to serve.

baked goods. Wild rice actually comes from a reed-like aquatic plant, which is unrelated to the rice seed. Wild rice has a nutty flavor and a chewy texture, is long and black to brown in color, and can be prepared like traditional rice and used in the same manner.

Couscous is made from ground semolina and comes in degrees of coarseness, medium-fine being the most popular. It is prepared by pouring over boiling stock or water and allowing the small pellets to swell as they absorb the liquid. You serve it in the same way as you would rice.

Barley is normally purchased as "pearled" barley, which has had the outer bran removed. It is commonly used in soups and stews and can be served as rice, although it has a longer cooking time. Barley is one of the oldest grains known to humankind; it is extremely hardy, growing in tropical to arctic climates. Most of the barley crops produced around the world are used for making beer. Barley has a sweet, earthy flavor and soft, chewy texture.

Oats are most familiar as a breakfast cereal. Steel-cut oats are whole grains that have been cut into small pieces with steel blades, resembling cracked wheat. Rolled oats are whole grains that have been steamed and flattened between rollers, a process that reduces cooking time. Instant oats are partially cooked, dried, and rolled so that they need only to be rehydrated in boiling water.

Quinoa *(keen-wa)* was a common food to the Incas of the Andes and was also referred to as the "mother grain," although it is not a true grain. Quinoa is very high in protein and lower in carbohydrates than other grains. It is a tiny ivory-colored grain with a mild flavor. Before cooking, wash and drain well to remove the bitter coating that occurs naturally on the grain. Quinoa is a gluten-free product and is suitable for anyone who is concerned about wheat allergies. Cook and serve it just as you would rice.

Tabouleh
Bulgar is a cracked wheat with a nutty flavor and light, fluffy texture; perfect to make this Middle East favorite.

82 | Legumes

Legumes are a staple of any vegetarian diet and are an essential part of many cuisines around the world. They are versatile, nutritious, economical, and, if dried, have a long shelflife.

Aduki beans

Black beans

Black-eyed beans

Borlotti beans

Butter beans

Canellini beans

Chick peas

Dried peas

Lentils

Haricot beans

Flageolet beans

Kidney beans

Split peas

Pinto beans

Soy beans

Legumes are plants that have double-seamed pods containing a single row of seeds. Of the hundreds of known varieties of bean, some are used for their edible pods, others for shelling fresh, and some for their dried seeds only. Beans, peas, lentils, and peanuts are among the most common legumes used by chefs. In many countries it is more common to eat dried beans, usually with rice, than meat or fish for daily protein; they are also rich in B-vitamins and minerals. With the growth of vegetarianism and veganism over recent decades, legumes are much in demand by customers.

Fresh beans

This category includes green beans, runner beans, or snap beans that can be eaten whole once the stem has been removed. Also included are haricot verts, which are long, slender pods with an intense flavor. The beans may be left whole, cut lengthwise, or cut on the diagonal. Make sure you remove the string running along the stem before cooking. Beans that should have their pods removed before eating include fava, lima beans, and flageolets; their pods are too tough and are normally removed before cooking.

The best season to buy fresh beans is from April through December. Look for beans that have a bright color, without brown areas or soft spots, and which are medium in size, since they can become tough if they have been allowed to grow too large. You can also buy them canned, pickled, or frozen. Most fresh beans can be steamed, boiled, microwaved, or sautéed.

111 Workout: Soaking dried beans

The most economical way to buy legumes is in their dried form, which means that they have to be rehydrated before cooking. The exception to the rule are split peas and lentils, which can be cooked without soaking.

1 Pick through the beans removing grit, small pebbles, or other debris.

2 Pour water over and remove skins that float to the surface. Drain.

3 Place the beans in a bowl and soak for several hours or overnight.

4 Drain the beans, the soaking water can be used in the recipe or discarded.

Dried legumes

Common dried beans and peas include split green peas, black beans, black-eyed peas, red kidney beans, pinto beans, and lentils. Shape is the best indicator for identification: beans are oval- or kidney-shaped; lentils are small, flat disks; and peas are round. Beans and peas that are dried are left on the vine until fully matured then harvested, shelled, and dried in warm air currents.

You can buy dried beans and peas in bags or in bulk. They should be stored in a cool, dry place. Do not refrigerate. You can buy many varieties of beans and peas that have been cooked, canned, or frozen. They can also be turned into flour, oil, or bean curd. Lentils

112 Workout:
Quick-soaking method

This method avoids the need to soak the beans overnight. Pick through the beans and rinse them. After quick-soaking, cook the beans according to your recipe.

1 Place the beans in a large saucepan and pour over fresh cold water, covering them by about 2 in (5 cm) of water.

2 Place the saucepan on the stove and bring to the boil then simmer for two to three minutes. Remove from the heat and cover with a lid.

3 Let the beans soak covered for one hour, then drain them. Remember that red kidney beans need to be boiled for at least ten minutes to degrade toxins.

and split peas do not need soaking, but most other dried beans do need to be soaked before cooking. Soaking rehydrates the beans, which, in turn, reduces the cooking time. Beans can be simmered in stock or water or baked in a liquid until they are soft and tender. You can eat them on their own or with rice or bread.

Fresh shelling peas

Among the most commonly used are the English pea or green garden pea, with the French petit pois coming a close second place. Most shelling peas are sold frozen or canned because they rapidly lose their flavor and color once shelled. A very popular bean in America and Asia is the soybean, or edamame, which is served as a snack in many sushi restaurants and is high in protein, fiber, and phytochemicals.

Green peas are best bought in the shell, which should be firm, without any brown spots, and have a bright green color. They should have a delicate, sweet flavor, eaten raw or cooked. The best way to cook them is by steaming them until they are tender, but they can be braised with meats such as ham or served as a vegetable garnish or in salads. Soybeans should have a light green fuzzy pod enclosing a tender, sweet pea, and are best steamed or processed into oil, tofu, or stir-fry sauces.

Edible pea pods

The best known are snow peas, sugar snap peas, and pea shoots, which can all be eaten raw or cooked. When preparing snow peas it is important to remove the string that runs along the stem, whether you are eating them raw, steamed, or stir-fried. Sugar snap peas are a cross between the garden pea and the snow pea—again eaten whole so do not try to shell them before cooking. The best season to buy them is March to April, but they can be bought through most of the year. Don't buy them if they are shriveled in appearance or covered with brown spots. Pea shoots are used in stir-fries or in the same way as other leafy vegetables.

Grow your own
Try growing your own vegetables. This might sound difficult, but most top chefs maintain their own vegetable patches. This means that they know exactly where the vegetables have come from and what has been used on them to grow the size and shape desired for their restaurant. You don't have to have a big garden; start small and see how it goes.

A wonderful vegetable
Legumes are a group of vegetables that include beans, peas, and lentils. This incredible family of vegetables has met the needs of human nutrition for centuries: legumes are easy to grow, a great source of protein, and, when dried, will last a lifetime.

Sweeteners, fats, & oils

Sugar, along with salt, was once a symbol of prosperity and wealth, and it is now widely used in many aspects of food preparation.

Sugar is responsible for balancing acidity in foods, contributing to appearance and flavor, as well as retaining moisture and prolonging freshness and shelflife.

Sweeteners

"Refined" sugars (sucrose) cover the categories of granulated sugar, fine sugar, or table sugar. Very fine and superfine sugars are finer than granulated sugar and are used in most baked goods since they hold higher amounts of fat when blended. Sanding sugar has a very coarse grain and is used to coat cakes and donuts. Icing, confectioner's, or powdered sugars are very fine sugars used to make royal icing for piping cakes.

Corn and glucose syrup

Used mainly for retaining moisture in food, corn syrup is widely used in commercial products. In the kitchen it may be used to make cake icings. It is made by converting corn starch into a simple sugar syrup using mainly glucose with the addition of other sugars. It is made from pure glucose sugar.

Honey, molasses, and brown sugar

Honey is used mainly for its flavor, which can vary considerably according to the nectar brought back to the hive. More expensive than other sugars, it remains smooth and resists crystallizing because of an acid it contains. It is a mixture of glucose and fructose.

Molasses comes from concentrated sugar-cane juice, which contains large amounts of sucrose and other sugars, acids, and impurities. Brown sugar is mostly sucrose with varying amounts of molasses; the darker the color, the more molasses it contains. Both molasses and brown sugar are mainly used in baked goods.

Cooking sugar

Sugar can be added to most items in its dry state or first liquefied into a syrup. There are two types of sugar syrups: simple syrup, which is a mixture of sugar and water, and cooked syrups, which are made of melted sugar cooked until it reaches a specific temperature.

Stages of cooked sugar

Stage	Temperature
Thread	236°F (113°C)
Soft ball	240°F (116°C)
Firm ball	246°F (119°C)
Hard ball	260°F (127°C)
Soft crack	270°F (132°C)
Hard crack	300°F (149°C)
Caramel	338°F (170°C)

Note: you need a sugar/candy thermometer that can measure very high temperatures.

Brown sugar

Coarse sugar

Confectioner's sugar

Corn syrup

Honey

Molasses

113 Workout: How to make a simple stock syrup

Simple stock syrups and cooked sugars are solutions of water and sugar boiled together and are used to make sauces, sorbets, and beverages. Cooked sugar for caramel sauce, meringue, buttercream, and candy requires a higher cooking temperature than a simple sugar. You will need a sugar/candy thermometer that measures very high temperatures to make sure the concentration of sugar is accurate.

1 Always use a heavy, clean saucepan, preferably copper. Stir the solution of sugar and water until it dissolves.

2 On boiling, brush the sides with cold water. Place in the thermometer. Cook until the desired stage is reached.

Fats

Fat is a food group that includes butter, lard, margarine, shortening, and oil. These items provide flavor, color, moisture, and richness, and assist with leavening in baked goods; they are solid at room temperature, while oils are liquid.

Butter

Butter is most commonly used to add flavor, richness, and smoothness to the dish. It is made by mixing cream containing 30-45 percent milk fat at high speeds. The finished butter must contain at least 80 percent butterfat and the remaining 20 percent is made up of milk solids and water. Sweet butter is made from pasteurized fresh cream. It is pale yellow in color and can be salted or unsalted. Butter is good for cooking as it adds color and flavor; it is often clarified, involving removing the milk solids and water, giving the butter a higher smoke point, which makes it less likely to burn when heated.

Lard and shortenings

Lard is almost 100 percent fat, is white in color, with only a small amount of water. It is made by rendering pork fat and is good for yielding flaky, tasty pastries. Shortenings are made from 100 percent fat and/or vegetable oils that are solidified through hydrogenation. They are ideal for using in baked goods because they are flavorless, with a relatively high melting point.

Oils

Oils come from various seeds, plants, and vegetables and remain liquid at room temperature. Each oil has its own flavor, aroma, and cooking properties.

Vegetable oil

Vegetable oil is extracted from a variety of plants, including corn, peanut, rapeseeds, and soybeans. Vegetable oils are virtually odorless and neutral in flavor. Because they are made without animal products they are cholesterol-free. If they are labeled "pure" then they contain one type of oil. Those labeled "vegetable oil" contain several blends of oil. Salad oil is a highly refined blend of oils.

Canola oil

This has a very high smoke point, with no flavor, so it is good for frying and cooking. It is made from rapeseeds and contains no cholesterol.

Nut oils

Packaged as "pure," since nut oils are never blended, they should have a strong flavor and aroma of the nut of origin. Examples are walnut or hazelnut, which are generally used to make salad dressings. Nut oils are not usually used to cook with, because their flavor is diminished with heat and they tend to go rancid quickly.

Olive oil

Olive oil is the only oil that is extracted from the fruit rather than the seed, nut, or plant. Like wine, olive oil comes in many different flavors and colors. "Extra virgin," "virgin," and "pure"

Melting points of fats

Stage	Temperature
Butter, whole	92°F-98°F (33°C-36°C)
Butter, clarified	92°F-98°F (33°C-36°C)
Cocoa butter	88°F-93°F (31°C-34°C)
Lard	89°F-98°F (32°C-36°C)
Margarine, solid	94°F-98°F (34°C-36°C)
Shortening, vegetable	120°F (49°C)
Shortening, emulsified vegetable	115°F (46°C)
Shortening, heavy-duty fryer	97°F-107°F (36°C-42°C)

refer to the amount of acidity of the oil; the less acidity the better quality the oil. Virgin is 100 percent unadulterated olive oil that has been cold-pressed. "Extra virgin" means that the oil has no more than 1 percent acidity, while virgin may have up to 3 percent acidity. "Pure" is made after the first pressing of the olives, using the leftover pulp.

Sesame oil

This oil is produced in India from the seeds of a large native annual herb, which has a nutty, slightly bitter, flavor. Toasted sesame oil is used as a condiment or as a flavoring in Chinese, Japanese, and Korean dishes, while the untoasted, milder, oil is used in Mediterranean and Indian cooking.

Infused or flavored oils

Basil, rosemary, parsley, garlic, citrus, and spice can all flavor oils that may be used to dip bread or make marinades, salad dressings, sauces and as a cooking medium. Oils generally used are olive oil or canola.

114 Workout: Preparing a basil-flavored oil

Chop a handful of basil leaves and place them in a jar with a screw-top lid. Pour in some olive oil and put the lid on. Allow the oil to stand for up to 24 hours. Shake the jar periodically to obtain the best flavor from the basil. Strain, clean the jar, and pour the flavored oil back into it, keeping it in the refrigerator until you need it. Use the oil on salads or to dip fresh, crusty bread in as an appetizer before a meal.

You must store flavored oils in the refrigerator. Raw herbs and fresh garlic or other fresh ingredients are potentially hazardous if you don't keep them refrigerated.

Preparing vegetables

The quickest and easiest way to practice your cuts is on vegetables and herbs. This means that you can learn on something that is cheap to buy and good to eat, and you can use the trimmings to add to your soups or stews. The vegetable cuts and herbs will enhance the presentation of your entrées or salads.

Key knife safety points

- Use the correct knife for cutting vegetables.
- Always cut away from yourself.
- Cut vegetables on a chopping board made of plastic or wood, not glass, marble, or metal.
- Place a clean, damp cloth or paper towel under your board to stop it from sliding.
- Keep knives sharp, as they are more dangerous when dull since you need to apply more pressure to cut.
- If carrying a knife around the kitchen, walk holding it close to your leg, pointing down and blade facing behind.
- Never attempt to catch a falling knife. Step back and let it fall to the floor.
- Never leave your knives in the sink unattended; this could cause injury.
- Do not wash your knives in a dishwasher. The heat and chemicals can damage the edge and handle. They could also injure someone removing them from the dishwasher.

115 Workout: Washing vegetables to be peeled

In a commercial kitchen you wash all the vegetables in a vegetable sink. Using a bowl to wash and another for your peelings will do the job at home.

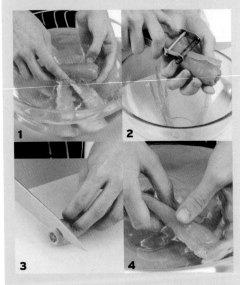

1 Take a bowl and fill with cold water; wash the vegetables to remove any surface dirt.
2 Remove from the water and, using your peeler, remove a thin layer of peel into another bowl.
3 Remove any unwanted areas from the vegetables by cutting with your knife.
4 Rewash the vegetables.

Your cutting station

You will need your knife kit, a chopping board, washed vegetables and herbs, and some containers for your cuts, trimmings, and waste. Remember to periodically hone your knife blade with your steel as you work; this will keep it sharp and aligned.

Preparing vegetables for cutting

Before you peel the vegetables, make sure you wash them first. This will remove any surface dirt and bacteria and any other contaminants that might come in contact with the cut surface during preparation. Rinse herbs under cold running water, then shake off excess water, and pat them dry with paper towels.

116 Workout: Washing leeks

Dirt gets trapped between the leaves and needs to be removed. If really dirty, leave to soak; this will soften and dislodge the dirt.

1 Place the leek on your chopping board and cut in half lengthwise all the way from root to top.
2 Using your fingers, gently separate the leaves and wash any grit or dirt that is hidden under the layers. The root will hold everything together.

Heel
The heel can be used for chopping vegetables finely or carrying out coarse work.

Center
The center of the blade is used for most of the general work when cutting vegetables.

Tip
The tip is where the knife is at its thinnest and narrowest. It can be used on small or delicate vegetable items.

117 Workout: Using a vegetable peeler

Vegetable peelers do a better job than a knife at removing the thin layer of skin from vegetables and fruits. Asparagus, carrots, parsnips, and potatoes are all good examples of vegetables that are best peeled with a peeler as you don't take much of the edible flesh of the product away. Remember that most nutrients are found just beneath the skin, so you don't want to throw that away by taking too much flesh with the skin.

118 Workout: Peeling with a knife

You can use your paring knife to peel thick-skinned vegetables and fruits such as grapefruits, oranges, or onions. Larger vegetables and fruits, such as winter squash or pineapples, need a large knife: your chef's knife is the best choice here. Make sure you cut off the top and bottom of the fruit or vegetable before peeling, to give yourself a flat, stable end to work with. This will prevent the item from moving around on your chopping board.

119 Workout: Peeling asparagus

Asparagus has a woody part to the stalk, which can easily be snapped off with your fingers. Then, using your peeler, gently remove a thin layer of peel away from the base of the asparagus. You can also use your paring knife held at a 20-degree angle to shave off the peel.

Basic cuts and shapes

If necessary, remind yourself about how to hold the knife (see page 23) before you start. It is very important to learn the basic cuts you will need when going to college or working in any kitchen around the world, so the more practice you can get cutting vegetables, the better.

Learning to cut and shape food products into uniform sizes is important for enhancing the appearance of the product and ensuring even cooking. Try the following vegetable cuts: chopping (to cut into irregularly shaped pieces); mincing (to chop into very fine pieces); chiffonade *(shi-foe-nod)* shredding (usually lettuce or large leaf herbs).

120 Workout: Chopping

Gather the herbs into a tight ball before slicing through them. Use your guiding hand to hold them in position (**1**). Once you have started to chop through the herbs, hold the tip of your knife with your guiding hand (**2**) and rock the knife back and forth to coarsely chop the herbs.

121 Workout: Slicing

Start the knife with the tip on the board. Move the knife forward and down to slice through. Finish with the knife against the board, raise the heel off the board, and rock the blade forward to make your second cut. The blade should never leave the board.

122 Workout: Mincing

Mincing is taking chopping to the next level. It's a very fine cut, which is suitable for many vegetables and herbs such as onions, shallots, garlic, and parsley. After chopping, rock your knife back and forth until you have achieved a very fine cut.

88 | Cutting vegetables

One of the most important tools that any student must master is the knife, and this is particularly important in vegetable preparation. To become a true professional chef, you must become skilled at using your knives and knowing which one to use. Every chef at the start of his or her professional life spends hours making julienne, bâtonnet, dicing, paysanne, and turning vegetables. Learning to perform these basic cuts safely and efficiently is an essential part of chef training.

We have already discussed how to select your knife set, hold a knife, and keep a sharp edge to your knives (see pages 22-23). In the previous section we started knife cuts on vegetables; we now take that one step further and continue with some classic cuts, which in any professional kitchen will be called by their French name, such as julienne, which refers to matchstick shapes.

Learning to control your knife is essential to producing even cuts. You must control your knife with one hand and hold the item being cut with the other; the sharp edge of the blade should cut through the food item. Never force the blade through, as this could cause an accident. Forcing means that your knife is dull, so always make sure it is sharp. Take your time; speed will come later. Use smooth, even strokes and make sure that your cuts are even, which helps cooking; the pieces will all cook at the same time if they have been cut to the same size and shape.

123 Workout: Dicing vegetables

To get the best flavor from onions, prepare them just before using; this will retain as much flavor as possible. The best method to stop the tears flowing when cutting onions is to use the sharpest knife possible. A blunt knife bursts the onion, which then releases a substance in the onion called allyl sulfide, which affects your eyes.

1 Cut through the root, giving two equal halves. Start by cutting through the onion lengthwise.

2 Slice through the onion in even widths, but not all the way to the end of the onion.

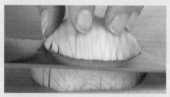

3 Turn the onion and make three horizontal cuts into it.

4 Now cut vertically down through the onion to the board, making small or large dice.

124 Workout: Cutting bâtonnet

1 Block off the carrot to a 2-in (5-cm) length. Then cut into 1/4-inch (6-mm) slices.
2 Cut further into 1/4-inch (6-mm) strips, giving you uniform-shaped bâtonnet of 1/4 x 1/4 x 2 in (6 x 6 x 50 mm).

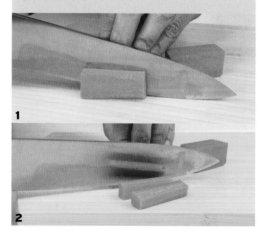

Basic cuts and shapes

Learning to cut and shape food products into uniform sizes is important for two main reasons; it enhances the appearance of the product and ensures even cooking.

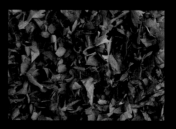

Chop: to cut an item into irregularly shaped pieces.

Mince: to chop an item into very fine pieces.

125 Workout: Cutting fine julienne

Julienne is normally ⅛ x ⅛ x 2 in (3 x 3 x 50 mm), but when using leeks the thickness is even smaller, making a fine julienne, which can be used for deep-frying and serving with fish and shellfish dishes, creating a dramatic effect.

1

2

3

Vegetable sizing chart

This gives an idea of the relative size of different vegetable cuts to aim for. Make your own chart, photocopy and laminate it, and lay your cut vegetables on top. Measurements are in inches.

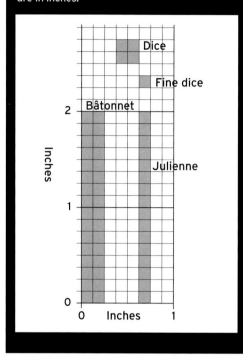

Dice

Fine dice

Bâtonnet

Julienne

Inches

2

1

0

0   Inches   1

126 Workout: Cutting paysanne

1

2

3

1 Square off the carrot with your knife until you have four even sides which are ½ in (1 cm) square.
2 Then cut into ⅛-in (3-mm) thick strips.
3 Cut each strip in ½-in (1-cm) squares, leaving you with paysanne ½ x ½ x ⅛ in (1 cm x 1 cm x 3 mm).

127 Workout: Cutting tourné

Tourné is a cutting technique that results in a 2 in (5 cm) barrel shape with seven equal sides and flat ends. It is worth practicing this method over and over again to achieve great results that are consistent every time.

1 Start by blocking off the carrot to a rectangle shape. Then start cutting from the top of the carrot close to the center.

2 Bring your turning knife or paring knife from the center and curve out to the side, keeping it as uniform as possible.

3 Continue to turn on all sides, carving from the top to the bottom.

4 You are aiming for seven even, smooth sides that have a uniform barrel shape.

Chiffonade: to finely slice or shred an item, usually lettuce or large-leaf herbs.

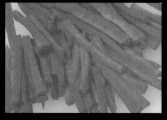

Julienne and bâtonnet: thin matchstick-shaped strips—both large and small.

Dicing: cubes of various sizes— brunoise, very small cubes, or small cubes.

Paysanne: flat squares

Boiling & steaming vegetables

Boiling and steaming are the two most frequently used techniques for cooking vegetables. They are easy to carry out, are economically sound for the kitchen, and adapt easily to a great many finished preparations.

The importance of vegetables
Vegetables are as much a focal point of a dish as the main food on the plate; they add color and texture to the finished dish. Buy them at their peak of quality, store, and handle them properly, paying attention to their preparation and cooking.

Boiling technique
Almost all vegetables can be boiled, and this is probably the easiest cooking method, yet it still results in a wide range of textures and flavors. You can use boiling to blanche, par-cook, or fully cook vegetables. The vegetables can then be served hot or chilled down and served cold in a salad, glazed in butter or olive oil, turned into a purée, or added to a stew or braised dish, or served in their own right or as a side dish.

Prepare your vegetables by rinsing in cold running water and scrubbing the vegetables to remove any dirt. Then peel the skin, if you are unable to leave it on, and trim it to an even size, shape, and diameter to ensure even cooking, or you can leave it whole. Vegetables that have a tendency to oxidize (turn brown with exposure to air), such as artichokes, need to be rubbed with lemon juice or placed in acidulated water (water and lemon juice) before cooking. However, leaving vegetables in water for extended periods robs them of their flavor, texture, and all-important nutrients.

Choose a pan large enough to hold the vegetables (do not overcrowd the pan; the water needs to circulate around the vegetables to cook them evenly), leaving enough room for the water to expand when heated. Add salt and any other aromatics you are using. Placing a lid on the pan will shorten cooking time, but is not essential. Make sure you check the vegetables regularly to avoid overcooking them. Most vegetables are added to boiling water, except starchy root vegetables such as turnips, celeriac, or new potatoes, which are normally started in cold water. Bring the water back to boiling, then turn

down the temperature to a simmer so that the vegetables do not break.

To help retain the color of certain vegetables, such as red cabbage, orange- and yellow-colored vegetables, or beets, bring the water back to a boil and cover with a lid. This will retain the acids in the vegetables and set the color. Leave green vegetables, such as broccoli, uncovered to retain color. Cook vegetables to their appropriate doneness, then strain and serve immediately or shock in iced water to arrest the cooking process, remove from the water, and store in a covered container in the refrigerator until needed.

Steaming technique
Any vegetable that can be boiled can also be steamed. This technique retains considerably more nutrients than boiling since nutrients can be lost in the water if cooked for too long. Steaming also retains good color and vegetables normally have a firmer texture. Steaming cooks

129 Workout: **Steaming broccoli**

Take two heads of broccoli, wash, and trim down the stems with a vegetable peeler before rewashing. Place the heads in the top pan of a double steamer and season with sea salt and freshly ground black pepper. Bring the water in the bottom pan to a rapid boil. Place the lid over the broccoli and steam the broccoli for five to seven minutes. Remove it from the steamer, taste, and adjust the seasoning if necessary. Serve immediately or chill down and store for later use.

128 Workout: **Boiling vegetables**

Take a saucepan large enough to hold the required amount of vegetables that you are boiling, fill with water, and season with salt and any other seasonings or aromatic ingredients. Make sure you use enough water to cover the vegetables comfortably. Bring the water to a boil and add the vegetables. Once the vegetables have been added, bring the water back to a rapid simmer and cook them until they have reached the appropriate level of doneness.

130 Workout: Cooking chick peas

Most legumes need to be soaked overnight, with the exception of lentils and split peas. Pick through the beans or peas and remove any dirt or other impurities. Rinse under cold running water, then place them in a large bowl and cover by at least 1 in (2.5 cm) of water; soak for at least six to eight hours, or overnight, to rehydrate.

1 Drain the beans or peas and rinse well. Place in a large saucepan and cover with cold water (3 parts water to 1 part legumes).

2 Bring to a boil and boil for ten minutes, then simmer for 40-45 minutes, depending on the type and age of the legume.

3 Squeeze the legume between your fingers and thumb to test for doneness. They should be firm to soft, but still intact, with the skin on.

the vegetables in a vapor bath, which is a direct heat, so cooking times can be very short.

Prepare the vegetables as you would for boiling. The liquid used is normally water, but you can use fresh stocks or a good-quality broth to enhance flavor. You can cook small amounts in an insert pan or larger amounts in a tiered steamer, pressure steamer, or convection steamer. As for boiling, you need enough room for the steam to circulate around the food for it to cook evenly. It is easy to overcook vegetables by steaming, and this is a common mistake. Once cooked, serve or store as you would boiled vegetables.

You can also pan-steam vegetables by cooking them in a covered pan with a small amount of liquid; most of the cooking is done by the steam because only a small portion of the food is submerged.

When you are steaming you can replace some of the water with fresh stock, broth, fruit juice such as orange or apple, or add aromatics to flavor the steaming liquid, such as carrots, onions, garlic, celery, or leeks. In addition, consider adding herbs and spices to the steamed liquids, such as bay leaf, ginger, parsley, garlic, thyme, cilantro, and black peppercorns.

Other techniques

Blanching is when you immerse vegetables in boiling water for between 30 seconds and one minute to remove the skin.

Par-cooking or **par-boiling** is to part-cook food items that will be finished by grilling, sautéeing, or stewing later. The aim is to eliminate or reduce strong odors or flavors.

Shocking or **refreshing** is when you submerge the food in ice-cold water to quickly cool or to stop the cooking process. The aim is to set the color of the food.

Al dente means "firm to the bite" or "to the tooth," meaning that the food offers a slight resistance in texture. This serves as the first step before other cooking techniques.

Moist-heat cooking methods

All these methods use water or steam to transfer heat, emphasizing the natural flavors of foods.

Term	Method
Boiling	convection transfers heat from hot liquid to the food at approximately 212°F (100°C)
Poaching	food cooks in simmering liquid at 160°F-185°F (71°C-82°C)
Simmering	convection transfers heat from a hot liquid by submersion at approximately 185°F-205°F (85°C-96°C)
Steaming	food is cooked in a vapor bath in which heat is transferred by hot steam by direct contact

131 Workout: How to cook rice

The basic formula for rice is one part rice to two parts water. Bring the correct amount of water to a boil in a saucepan and season with salt. Add the rice. Cover the pan with a lid and reduce the heat to a simmer. Cook the rice until all the water has been absorbed and the rice is tender. This will take approximately 15 minutes. Strain the rice into a colander to allow excess moisture to drain. Serve.

Stewing, roasting, & frying vegetables

Having your vegetable preparation area set up properly will help you feel efficient and professional as a chef. Collect all your ingredients and tools together, then everything will be in its place to start all your different cooking methods.

Roast tomatoes
Tomatoes lightly roasted in oil make a delicious accompaniment to any roast-meat dish.

Sautéeing and pan-frying

For sautéeing you use a little fat and high heat and flip the food, while for pan-frying you use a larger amount of fat and longer cooking time. You can cook vegetables from raw with both methods, but usually both methods are used to reheat precooked vegetables. You can glaze vegetables during sautéeing by adding a little butter, sugar, or honey to coat them as they reheat. Stir-frying is similar to sautéeing, but you stir the vegetables as they cook.

Baking and roasting

Baking vegetables such as potatoes, squash, or sweet potatoes produces a dense, dry texture. Unlike boiling or steaming, the texture is much firmer. You can also bake other vegetables such as tomatoes, eggplant, red onions, and turnips. The dry heat caramelizes the sugars in the vegetables, giving an intense flavor. The term "roasted" can be used to describe the dish. Marinades can enhance flavor and give extra protection to the vegetable in dry heat.

Broiling

Peppers, zucchini, mushrooms, eggplant, onions, and corn can all be successfully broiled. The intense heat gives vegetables rich, bold flavors. Pick fresh, firm vegetables—those that are soft and wilting are not the best choice. Wash, trim and cut them into even sizes, brush with a little fat, and cook until lightly browned. Broiled vegetables are often served with salads or coated with olive oil or a light vinaigrette. Large vegetables normally need to be partially cooked before being finished by broiling. Broiling can also be used to finish off certain dishes, such as casseroles or gratins, to give a pleasing color.

132 Workout: Preparing a vegetable stir-fry

A stir-fry should be quick and easy to make. Start by selecting your vegetables, then rinse, trim, and peel them and cut them into even sizes. Select a cooking fat to complement the flavor of the vegetables. Oils such as olive, peanut, canola, corn, or safflower are all good choices.

1 Start by heating the wok, then add the oil and swirl around the sides of the wok. Add the vegetables that will take the longest to cook first.

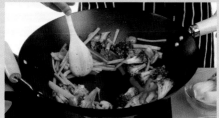

2 Stir-fry means exactly that! Stir the vegetables as they fry. If you leave them to sit in the oil they begin to steam and will go soft.

3 Keep adding vegetables, moving them around the wok. Constant stirring keeps the oil hot, frying the food evenly.

4 Add vegetables such as zucchini at the midpoint and the vegetables that require the least cooking, such as mangetout, toward the end.

5 Tender ingredients can be added last. Some vegetables may become tender while others remain crisp. Add seasonings and serve very hot.

Deep-frying

Deep-frying results in a crisp texture on the outside and a firm, light center on the inside, depending on thickness. Vegetables can be breaded and battered, or tempura, dipped in a very light batter, which highlights fresh, crisp vegetables. Choose oils such as vegetable oil, corn oil, canola, and safflower oil that have high smoke points and neutral flavor. Use paper towels to blot excess fat.

Braising and stewing

Braising and stewing could be used on one item or a combination. Prepare vegetables normally, leaving them whole or in large pieces for a braise and in small pieces to stew. You can also use aromatic ingredients, such as a mirepoix, to add flavor as the stewed or braised vegetables cook in their own juices. You may add a thickening agent to the liquid to add body to the sauce.

133 Workout: Pan-frying

Pan-frying is similar to sautéeing, only you are using more oil in the pan. Rinse, peel, and cut the vegetables into even sizes. If necessary coat them with bread mix, flour, or batter.

1 Heat the oil until it is hazy or shimmering. Add the vegetables without overcrowding the pan.

2 Cook over medium heat until the vegetables become lightly browned. Turn them to finish, remove from the pan, place on paper towel. Season and serve.

134 Workout: Making a ratatouille

Ratatouille is a very robust peasant stew from France that merges several different vegetables together. These can include eggplant, yellow, red, and green peppers, tomatoes, garlic, onions, zucchini, mushrooms, tomato paste, and stock. Together they make a wonderful, richly flavored, full-bodied vegetable dish.

1 Start by using a large saucepan or rondeau. Heat the oil until hot, then add the onions and garlic, and sauté until translucent.

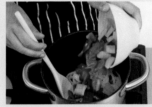

2 Lower the heat to medium, then add the tomato paste and coat the onions. Next add the mixed peppers.

3 Cook for a further three to four minutes, then add the eggplant and cook until it has softened.

4 Add the remaining vegetables in the following order: zucchini, mushrooms, and tomatoes. Cook each one until it has softened before adding the next.

5 Add the chicken or vegetable stock and allow the vegetables to stew. Taste and correct the seasoning.

6 The vegetables should be moist, but without resembling a soup consistency; tender and flavorful.

7 Add freshly chopped basil, parsley, or oregano. Taste and season, if necessary. Serve immediately.

Salads

Salads give the chef the chance to experiment with a rich mix of flavors, colors, and textures. Salads can be as simple as a green-leaf mix or comprise surprising combinations of leaves, vegetables, grains, or pasta, acting as a perfect accompaniment to meat, fish, or shellfish. Start simple and practice with a combination of leaves, seasoned and tossed with a simple vinaigrette.

Before the days of refrigeration most cold dishes were made in a cool pantry, before being brought into the hot kitchen to be sent into the dining room. The pantry was an ideal place for the kitchen team to produce great artistic displays for buffet presentations, from simple salads to pâtés and terrines to elaborate ice sculptures. Only a few years ago salads may have taken up one or two lines on the menu; now the choice is vast, sometimes occupying a whole page of a menu. Today's customers are more knowledgeable and health-conscious than those of the past, and demand a wide variety of freshly made salads served at their best.

Types of salads

Appetizer salad/first course should be designed to make an exciting first impression on your customer; they should stimulate the appetite and generate anticipation in the diner as to what will come next in the meal. This means that salads must have fresh, crisp ingredients, flavorful dressing, and an attractive appearance. Adding cheese, ham, cold cuts of meat, shrimp, or crab adds to this appeal. With the further addition of fresh or lightly cooked vegetables, these combinations of ingredients all help to create a stylish start to any meal.

Accompaniment salads are served with a main course, so they need to harmonize with the rest of the meal, such as any other side dish (vegetables). The accompaniment salad should be light and flavorful, bearing in mind what it is being served along with. You don't want to serve potato salad with a side dish of potato chips or French fries. Accompaniment salads are great to serve with a selection of sandwiches for a main course at lunch.

Entrée/main-course salads should be large enough to constitute a full meal and usually contain a substantial amount of protein in the form of meat, poultry, fish, or shellfish. For vegetarians, provide options including cheese, egg, tofu, or pulses. Health- and diet-conscious diners expect enough variety on the plate to form a balanced meal, both nutritionally and in flavor, freshness, and texture. This type of salad gives you an excellent opportunity to use your imagination and creativity to produce attractive, appetizing dishes full of color, texture, and flavor.

A separate course salad is meant to cleanse the palate after a rich main course or entrée and is served just before the dessert course. A few greens with light vinaigrette or a fruit salad are very popular choices here. The separate course

Green salads

Fresh greens must be clean, crisp, cold, and well drained of water. The use of moisture and air are necessary to keep them fresh. Wash your salad greens and drain them well. Leaves will wilt because they lose moisture. They will also lose flavor if left in water too long, but you can restore crispness by washing and refrigeration. Never pack them too tightly when storing—give them air to breathe, place in a colander with a drip tray underneath to catch any water, and cover with damp paper towels. Try not to prepare salad leaves too early as this will cause them to turn brown where they have been cut or torn.

Presentation guidelines

• Keep the salad away from the rim of the plate. Remember the waiter needs to pick the plate up and the customer does not want the waiter to touch their food.
• Try to add height to your salad; this adds attractiveness.
• Keep the salad simple—if it's too elaborate the customers may realize that too many hands have handled their food.
• Try to use as much color as possible in your salad; this will stimulate the appetite and give tremendous visual appeal.
• Practice your knife cuts and chop all the ingredients evenly and neatly. Aim for bite-size pieces.
• Make sure every ingredient is identifiable.

(135) Workout: Simple green salad

Wash some salad leaves and crisp them up by putting them back in the refrigerator for a short while. Then cut or tear the leaves into bite-size pieces unless you are using mesclun mix or mixed greens. Toss them together in a bowl and then add other green vegetables such as cucumber, green peppers, or string beans. Make sure they are all cut into evenly sized pieces. If serving immediately, add your dressing and toss well, covering all the ingredients. Then serve on a cold plate. Add a garnish such as a thin piece of toasted bread and serve.

salad was considered the norm on a menu in high-end restaurants a few years ago, but is not widespread these days.

Dessert salads mainly use fruit, with the addition of nuts, ice cream, and cream. They are too sweet to be served elsewhere on the menu.

Salad ingredients

These need to be as fresh as possible with lots of variety, color, and textures, but don't discount dried, frozen, or canned products.

Salad greens: romaine (cos), Boston, frisée (endive), spinach, micro greens, sprouts, arugula (rocket), radicchio, and edible flowers.

Fresh vegetables: avocado, broccoli, celery, cucumbers, mushrooms, bean sprouts, tomatoes, radishes, peppers, onions, artichokes, carrots, potatoes, and dried beans.

Cooked, canned, or pickled vegetables: corn, hearts of palms, olives, peas, pimientos, water chestnuts, artichoke hearts, and pickles.

Fruits—fresh, frozen, or canned: apples, berries, cherries, figs, grapefruit, kiwi, mangoes, melons, oranges, peaches, pears, prunes, and raisins.

Protein: cold cuts of meats, such as honey ham, Parma ham, salami, beef, chicken, turkey, as well as tuna, lobster, salmon, sardines, a variety of cheeses, eggs, tofu, nuts, and pulses.

Putting it all together

Most plated salads comprise four components: base, body, garnish, and dressing. A plated salad is not a salad buffet or salad made in bulk such as vegetable or potato salad.

The base is a layer of loose, whole, or shredded greens such as romaine or mixed greens. The body is usually the main ingredient, such as a chicken breast or lobster. The garnish adds texture and visual appeal; toasted bread or croutons, fresh fruit, or crisp vegetables. The dressing adds moistness, flavor, tartness, and sometimes spiciness, complementing the salad and main ingredient without overpowering it.

136 Workout: Cleaning salad leaves

Take care to remove all dirt from fresh salad leaves.

1 Fill a container large enough to accommodate the amount of leaves with fresh, cold water. Plunge the leaves in, shaking them to loosen any dirt.

2 Dry them in a salad spinner.

137 Workout: Making vinaigrette

A basic vinaigrette used as a salad dressing usually uses three parts oil to one part vinegar. Oils can be extra virgin olive oil, flavored oils, or corn oil. Mustard can be English, French, or whole grain. Start by mixing the mustard and any seasonings. Then whisk in the vinegar, slowly pour the oil into the mixture, and whip all the ingredients together. Adjust seasoning if necessary.

138 Workout: Making mayonnaise

1 Place egg yolks, mustard, and vinegar in a bowl and whip to combine well. Then slowly start adding the oil in a thin stream.

2 Continue to whisk the mixture together until all the oil has been incorporated.

3 Adjust the consistency by thinning with a small amount of water or lemon juice.

96 | Pasta

Pasta is Italian for "paste," which is basically what pasta is—made of wheat flour and liquid (water or oil). Some pastas may have eggs added to enrich the dough. Other ingredients may be used to give flavor, color, and texture.

Pasta has always been a staple food of the Italian diet, and is widely believed to have made the transition from Italy to other parts of Europe when Catherine de Medici married Henry II, the future king of France, in 1533. Thomas Jefferson is believed to have introduced America to Italy's popular food in the late 1700s, after he had lived in Paris and developed a taste for fresh pasta.

Pasta has traveled far beyond its original Italian borders to become one of the most popular foods on the planet—and this is not surprising. Only a few years ago the only pasta items on the average menu were macaroni cheese for the kids or spaghetti Bolognese for the adults. Now we know that the variety of pasta is almost endless—in shapes, sizes, sauces, and dishes. Easy to make, using inexpensive ingredients, nutritious, and versatile, you can adapt pasta to a number of uses right across the menu—from appetizers, entrées and salads to desserts.

An ancient food
How old is pasta? Records date back to the fifth century AD, when noodles appear in the Jerusalem Talmud, which makes reference to boiled noodles.

Dried pasta
The best dried pasta is made from semolina, which has a high protein content, taken from the inner part of durum wheat kernels. When buying dried pasta look for a good yellow color; the pasta itself should feel hard, brittle, and springy. It should snap cleanly. When cooked, pasta should hold its shape and be firm to the bite (al dente). Dried pasta can be made in different flavors by adding vegetable purées such as spinach, red pepper, tomato, and pumpkin. You can even find black pasta, made with the addition of squid ink; delicious with seafood.

Fresh pasta
Fresh pasta is made from all-purpose, or bread, flour, which is high in gluten and makes the pasta tender when cooked. Semolina is not the best flour to use when making fresh pasta, but is perfect for factory-made pasta. To make your own pasta use all-purpose flour with eggs or oil. Use your imagination and try adding vegetable purées and other flavoring to your freshly made pasta. Add herbs or spices, such as saffron, to give great taste and color, and citrus fruit for a zesty, tangy twist. You can also use other flours, along with all-purpose ones, such as cornmeal, rye, or buckwheat, all of which will give the pasta a different texture, flavor, and color.

Dried versus fresh
Which type is best? Both dried and fresh pasta have their own valuable properties. Fresh is best to use with cream-based sauces or butter; it also

World food
Pasta, noodles, and dumplings are eaten all around the world, and have been a staple since ancient times in Italy, the Middle East, and Asia. Pasta has traveled the globe since industrial production of this food began in the eighteenth century.

Pasta uses

Pasta	Common uses
Capelli	soups, broths
Conchiglie shells	soups, salads, stuffed
Farfalle	salads, soups
Fettuccine	cream sauces
Fusilli tricolori	shape, salads, soups
Lasagne	casseroles, bakes
Macaroni	creams, cheese sauces
Orzo	salads, soups
Penne	salads, casseroles
Ravioli	light sauces
Rigatoni	salads, casseroles
Spaghetti	light sauces, heavy sauces
Vermicelli	broths, soups, sauces

139 Workout: How to make fresh pasta

Pasta dough is one of the simplest products to make as it is basically flour and liquid mixed together. It is easy enough to make small batches of pasta, but you may need to use an electric mixer with a dough hook for larger batches. Making pasta by hand gives you the opportunity to work the dough until it is smooth and free of any lumps or dry spots, and this is a great learning experience for any chef.

1 Weigh out your flour. If you are using more than one kind, mix them together and make a well.

2 Break the eggs into a cup, then pour them into the center of the well and whisk with a spoon.

3 Now pour in the oil.

4 Lightly whisk the eggs again, only this time incorporate the oil to combine everything.

5 Using the spoon or your finger, pull in the flour from the sides of the well to start forming the dough.

6 Continue to incorporate the flour. You may need to use a bench scraper if the mixture sticks to the bench.

7 Using both hands, mix the flour into the liquid, rubbing your hands to loosen any dough.

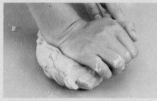

8 The mixture should be forming into a firm dough. Start to knead it together.

9 Using your palms, knead the dough until it becomes satiny. Then wrap it up in plastic wrap and rest it for at least 30 minutes.

absorbs more sauce than factory-dried pasta. The fresh version also gives you, the chef, the freedom to be creative, using your own special flavors, colors, and shapes. The downside is that fresh pasta has only a limited shelflife, though it can be frozen successfully. Dried pasta is ideal for olive oil, or tomato-based sauces, since it has a chewy and robust texture. In an Italian restaurant you'll find that chefs use both kinds on a regular basis.

As you gain experience and experiment with both fresh and dried pasta, you will get to know what works best with what sauce, what sauce clings best to which shaped pasta, or the way the pasta complements certain ingredients, such as fish, shellfish, poultry, or roasted vegetables. By changing the ratio of flour to liquid in fresh pasta and introducing other ingredients you can produce everything from a firm dough to a soft batter, which will handle and cook differently.

Knowing how to make the best use of pastas is something that all chefs need to experiment with, so trial and error is the best approach to take.

140 Workout: Pasta by hand

If you don't have a pasta machine, it's easy to roll out pasta by hand. Dust your bench with some flour or semolina and roll out the pasta as thinly as possible into one long sheet, using a rolling pin. Then roll it up into a long cylinder.

1 Place the cylinder on your chopping board and, using your paring knife, cut it into 1/8-in (0.3-cm) pieces for fettuccine, 1/4-in (0.6-cm) pieces for tagliatelle, and 1/2-in (1-cm) pieces for pappardelle.

2 Dry your noodles by hanging them from a pasta drying rack or by spreading them out on a clean dish cloth or paper towel.

Spaghetti

Lasagne

Penne rigate

Cannelloni

Farfalle

Macaroni

Fusilli tricolor

Tortelloni

Tagliatelli

Spirali

Ravioli

Conchiglie

All shapes and sizes
The huge variety of pasta shapes
and colors provides a great choice
to accompany and enhance any dish.

Angel-hair spaghetti

Campanelle

141 **Workout:** Using a pasta machine

Work with a small amount of
dough and hand-flatten it.

1 Set the pasta machine
on the widest setting and roll
the dough through it.

2 Lightly dust the dough with flour
or semolina.

3 Repeat the process of flouring
and rolling, folding the pasta over on
itself and rolling out again. This will
help keep the pasta an even shape.

4 Each time you pass the pasta
through the machine, tighten the
rollers until you get the required
thickness.

1

2

3

4

Pasta shapes

Pasta comes in all shapes and sizes. It varies from long, thin rods, strips, or ribbons of various widths to fancy shapes of all kinds and hollow tubes and shells. Long, thin rods, such as the familiar spaghetti, work well with a smooth tomato sauce or a rich cream sauce. Hollow tubes, such as penne or rigatoni, work well with robust, thick, chunky sauces. Thick pastas, such as pappardelle and farfalle, are the best choice if you are making an oven-baked dish, served with meat sauces. Large conchiglie (shells) can easily be filled with mushrooms or seafood. Fancy, ribbed pasta is great for trapping thick, hearty sauces, while a pasta with a smooth surface, such as fettuccine, is ideal as a vehicle for the lighter sauces made from bases such as cream, butter, or olive oil.

Stuffed pasta

Ravioli is the best-known stuffed pasta, and it is very easy to make. You simply lay the pasta sheet on your table and fill it with cheese and meat, which are the traditional Italian fillings, or you could try lobster, crabmeat, mushrooms, cheese, herbs, and a variety of vegetables (notably spinach and pumpkin). You lay another sheet of pasta on top, seal the edges, and cut into squares, circles, or triangles. Tortelloni is another type of stuffed pasta.

142 Workout: Cutting and drying tagliatelli

To turn your freshly made pasta into tagliatelli:

1 Roll the pasta out to a ⅛-in (0.3-cm) thickness. The pasta should feel smooth and not at all tacky.

2 Pass the pasta through the cutter roller attachment on the pasta machine, letting the cut noodles fall loosely onto the table. Dust the noodles with a little more flour or semolina to stop them sticking together.

3 Lay the tagliatelli to dry over a pasta rack.

Doneness serving

"To the bite," or as the Italians say "al dente," or perfectly cooked, pasta should be slightly firm to the bite. Cooking time varies according to its shape and thickness, and whether the pasta is fresh or dried. The best way to test to see if it is al dente is to take a small amount of the pasta and taste it; it should be tender but firm and not raw or doughy. When ready, remove from the heat, drain, and serve. The residual heat will continue to cook the pasta and keep it warm.

143 Workout: Preparing ravioli

Roll out two thin sheets of freshly made pasta, make your filling and either use a spoon, piping bag, or a small scoop to measure out the filling. To cut the pasta use a knife, pasta wheel, or cookie cutter.

1 Lay out your pasta. Using a spoon, deposit small portions of the filling on the dough.

3 Press around the filling to remove air pockets and seal the dough.

2 Carefully lay another thinly rolled-out sheet of pasta on top of the filling.

4 Use a pastry cutter to cut out each ravioli.

Cooking fresh and dried pasta

Freshly made pasta will cook in as little as two minutes, because of its high moisture content, while dried pasta, depending on thickness, will take between eight and twelve minutes to cook by boiling.

Boiling pasta

To boil pasta you really need at least 1 gallon (4 liters) of water for every 1 lb (500 g) of pasta, whether you are using the fresh or dried variety. Add 1 oz (28 g) of sea salt to the water. Bring the water to a boil, then add the pasta and stir, so that the pasta is completely submerged. Allow the water to come back to a rolling boil. The amount of water and its boiling motion will prevent the pasta from sticking together, but you will need to stir occasionally.

As soon as the pasta is firm, drain it in a large colander, move it to a serving dish, coat with your chosen sauce and serve immediately. If you are keeping the pasta for a later service, leave it in the colander under cold running water until it is completely chilled. Then drain and lightly coat with oil to stop it sticking together, place in a container, label, and store in the refrigerator until you need it.

Baked pasta

The best-known baked pasta dish is undoubtedly lasagne, which is a pasta casserole layered with other ingredients, such as meat, spinach, vegetables, and tomato sauce. Other pasta dishes, such as stuffed shells, can also be baked. On most occasions, baked pasta is precooked, assembled, and finished in the oven.

144 Workout: Boiling fresh pasta

Fill a large pot with cold water and place it on the stove. Bring the water to a rapid boil, and add salt. You don't need to add anything else to the water; the volume of water and its rapid movement will stop the pasta sticking together.

1 Pick up the fresh noodles in one hand and gently lower them into the rapidly boiling water.

2 As the noodles start to soften gradually push them completely into the water with a wooden spoon.

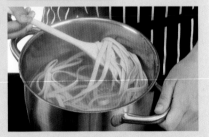

3 Stir the pasta around the pot to separate the strands and to stop it sticking to the bottom.

4 Bring the pasta back to a boil and cook until al dente. To test take your spoon and remove a small amount to taste.

145 Workout: Making and adding a cream sauce

Cream sauces work really well with spaghetti or fettuccini because the sauce sticks to the smooth surface of the pasta better than other types of pasta sauce, such as a thick, meaty sauce. The sauce shown here is based on bacon and cream and is a simple version of the traditional sauce known as carbonara.

1 Start with a clean frying pan. Heat some oil and add chopped bacon.

2 As the bacon crisps up, tip in the freshly cooked pasta and stir around the pan to stop it sticking to the bottom.

3 Pour in cream. As it comes to a boil reduce the heat so the sauce does not split. Stir to coat each strand of the pasta.

4 Add fresh herbs and seasoning, taste, and reseason if necessary. Portion equally between warmed pasta bowls, and serve.

Noodles & dumplings

Noodles are used in many Asian dishes and come in different shapes, sizes, textures, and flavors. Dumplings are another highly varied food that appears in a range of forms in European and Asian cuisines.

Asian noodles

Differences between the types of Asian noodles arise because of the flours and ingredients used to make the doughs. Most dried noodles need to be soaked in water before further preparation; the presoaking softens and separates the noodles, making them easier to cook evenly later.

Wheat noodles Known as "egg" noodles, wheat noodles are thin, flat, with a springy texture.

Bean starch and **buckwheat** Also known as cellophane, bean noodles, bean threads, and spring rain noodles, bean starch are thin, transparent noodles made from mung beans.

Rice noodles Also known as rice sticks, rice noodles are made with rice flour. They need to be soaked in hot water before you cook them, then rinsed in cold running water after boiling to remove excess starch. This will stop them sticking together. Rice noodles can be served in sautéed dishes or soups, or in the case of rice vermicelli, deep-fried and used as a garnish.

Dumplings

Dumplings can be sweet or savory and are small parcels made from dough, either steamed, simmered in stock or a flavored liquid, or shallow- or deep-fried. The popular Chinese dim sum include steamed yeast doughs and fried egg rolls, and some countries have specific dumpling dishes, such as Italian gnocchi, German spaetzle, Belorussian pelmeni, and Polish pierogi.

There are two main types of dumpling: one type is made with bread-like dough, served with stews, broths, or steamed and served with a dipping sauce as an appetizer or side dish. The other type is dumplings filled with meat, vegetables, cheese, or fruit. These use noodle dough or wrappers and are steamed, fried, or baked and served as appetizers or snacks.

Gnocchi Small dumplings made with a mixture of potato and wheat flour, with the addition of ricotta cheese or eggs and rolled into bite-sized pieces, gnocchi are boiled, then usually sautéed in butter and served with grated Parmesan.

Spaetzle Tiny dumplings, made from a thick batter of wheat flour, eggs, and milk, cream, or water. They are usually cooked by boiling in salted water, drained, then fried in butter and served as a side dish to braises and stews.

Types of Asian noodle

Type	Description	Use
Hokkien	egg and wheat noodles, resembles thick, yellow spaghetti	soups/stir-fried
Mian (mein)	Chinese wheat noodles, made with or without eggs; comes in different widths	soups/stir-fried deep-fried
Mung bean threads	very thin, gelatinous (cellophane) noodles made from mung beans	soups, salads, garnishes
Ramen	deep-fried noodles sold dried in packs with powdered seasoning (students love them)	stir-fried, soups
Flat rice noodles	made with rice flour; known by various names, depending on the country	noodle dishes such as Pad Thai
Soba	buckwheat or buckwheat and wheat noodles—chewy	salads/soups
Udon	thick Japanese flour noodles—soft and chewy	stews/stir-fried soups

146 Workout: How to make matzo balls

Try this easy preparation for matzo balls to liven up soups and stews.

Recipe
- 4 eggs, lightly beaten
- 4 oz (120 g) melted butter
- 5 tbs chicken fat, melted butter, or vegetable oil
- 2 fl oz (75 ml) stock or water
- 1 tsp salt
- ¼ tsp pepper
- Pinch of nutmeg (optional)
- 8 oz (240 g) matzo meal flour

1 Take a large bowl and lightly beat the eggs together, add the melted butter, stock, and dry ingredients.

2 Stir in the matzo meal flour and blend well together, cover the bowl with plastic wrap and place in the refrigerator for one hour to allow the dough to rest.

3 Remove the bowl from the refrigerator and shape the dough into small 1-in (2.5-cm) balls and drop them into simmering soup or stews. Cover the pan and simmer for 20 minutes before serving.

Dairy

Milk, cream, butter, cheese, and eggs are all delicious in their own right, but they are also key ingredients in many preparations. This section will help you learn why. You will also learn how dairy items are purchased and stored and why temperature control is so important. Dairy is a very small word, but it covers an enormous variety of products; learn the many varieties of milk, their fat content, and why it is one of the most nutritious foods available to humankind. You will also learn about the makeup of cream, from half-and-half to heavy, to the countless flavors, textures, aromas, and styles of cheese.

Eggs have two sections of their own, and rightly so, as eggs, particularly chicken's eggs, are an excellent food for humans, as they are high in protein, low in cost, and readily available. You will learn how to beat, whip, boil, poach, fry, scramble, and make pancakes and omelets. You will also learn about buying different sizes and grades, storing them, to finally realizing, as a chef, why eggs can be served at virtually any meal, any day of the week.

04 | Milk, cream, & butter

These dairy products, which come mainly from cow's milk, are extremely versatile and used throughout the kitchen. They can be served as they are or used as ingredients in a variety of dishes, from salads and soups to sauces and desserts.

Milk, cream, and butter provide texture, flavor, color, and nutritional value to every dish that they are added to.

Cow's milk

Cow's milk is one of the most nutritious foods available to humankind; it provides protein, vitamins, and minerals—it is an excellent source of calcium to build strong teeth and bones. Whole milk is approximately 88 percent water with around 3½ percent milk fat and 8½ percent other milk solids.

Types of milk processing

Pasteurization involves heating milk to a temperature of 161ºF (72ºC) for 15 seconds. This will kill any disease-causing bacteria and enzymes that cause the milk to spoil, thus prolonging its shelflife.

Ultra-pasteurization is mainly used with whipping cream and individual creamers to be added to hot beverages. The process involves heating the milk to 275ºF (135ºC) for two to four seconds. This high temperature and length of time destroys virtually all bacteria.

Ultra-high temperature (UHT) milk is held at a temperature of 280ºF–300ºF (138ºC-150ºC) for two to six seconds. It is then packed in sterile containers. You can store UHT at room temperature for at least three months, provided it remains unopened. It should be chilled before you open it and then stored in the same way as fresh milk, in the refrigerator. You should aim to use it within a few days of opening. UHT milk has a slightly cooked taste, but the high temperature of processing has little, if any, effect on the nutritional value of the milk.

Homogenization reduces the size of the fat cells in whole milk and permanently disperses them throughout the liquid. This prevents the fat from rising to the top of the milk, giving a more uniform consistency, a whiter color, and a richer taste to the milk.

Reduced fat is whole milk that has had milk fat reduced to 2 percent. Low-fat milk contains 1 percent milk fat. Non-fat milk, fat-free, no-fat, or skim milk contains less than half a percent milk fat.

Evaporated milk is whole homogenized milk with 60 percent of the water removed from it. It is then canned and heat-sterilized, which results in a cooked flavor and a darker color than fresh milk. It needs to be stored in a cool place, but once opened it should be treated just the same as fresh milk.

Butter

Butter (see also page 85) is firm at room temperature, but it starts to melt at 93ºF (33ºC) and reaches its smoke point at 260ºF (127ºC). Its flavor is unmatched in sauces, breads, and pastries. Clarified butter removes the water and milk solids to give a more stable product to use in cooking. As it achieves a higher smoke point, this process is called "clarification." Ghee is a form of clarified butter that originated in India. It also has a high smoke point and a nutty, caramel flavor.

147 Workout: Clarifying butter

Clarified butter is commonly used to make rouxs to thicken sauces, and to make warm butter sauces such as hollandaise and Béarnaise. It can also be used for sautéeing instead of vegetable oil or used in combination with vegetable oil to raise its smoking point. Use unsalted butter when clarifying butter, as salted butter will concentrate the salt in the butter.

1 Place the butter in a saucepan over low heat and slowly allow it to melt. Foam will begin to rise to the top.

2 Using a ladle, skim the foam from the top of the melted butter. The milk solids will fall to the bottom of the pan.

3 Remove the clarified butter, leaving the milk solids in the bottom.

148 Workout: Making buttercream

Buttercreams make delicious toppings and fillings for tortes, cakes, and pastry goods. They are made by blending butter with an egg and sugar base. You can make different icings by using whole eggs, egg yolks, or egg whites. Have your ingredients at hand, but keep eggs refrigerated until needed. Sift the sugar, soften the butter, and cut it into small cubes. You will also need a sugar/candy thermometer, spatula, and an electric mixer.

1 Combine sugar and water in a saucepan and bring to a boil. Use a wet pastry brush to wipe the sides of the pan. Cook the sugar until it reaches 240°F (116°C).

2 As the syrup is boiling whisk the egg whites to soft peak stage.

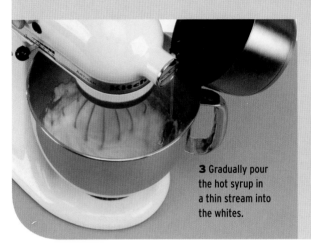

3 Gradually pour the hot syrup in a thin stream into the whites.

4 Add the softened butter in small amounts, continuing to whip until smooth.

5 Once the butter has been incorporated, it is ready to use or refrigerate.

Condensed milk is made from whole homogenized milk that has had 60 percent of the water removed, but it contains large amounts of sugar (40 to 45 percent). It is often used in desserts and confections.

Dry milk powder is made from pasteurized milk from which virtually all the liquid has been removed; the lack of moisture prevents the growth of microorganisms and extends shelflife. Add water to dry milk to use it like fresh milk, or use it in its dry form in bakery goods.

Types of cream

Cream contains at least 18 percent milk fat. It is slightly yellow or ivory in color and rich in flavor.

Half-and-half is composed of between 10 and 18 percent milk fat (fat content) and is a mixture of whole milk and cream. It is used in coffee or for breakfast cereal.

Single or **table cream** is composed of between 18 and 30 percent milk fat (fat content). It is frequently used in coffee, baked goods, or soups.

Whipping cream is made up of between 30 and 35 percent milk fat (fat content). It is often used

in baked goods, sauces, and in ice creams. It can be whipped into a foam and used in mousses.

Double or **heavy cream** is made up of not less than 36 percent milk fat and is used throughout the kitchen. When whipped it holds its texture longer than whipping cream.

Cultured dairy products

Yogurt is a thick, tart, pudding-like product made from milk cultured with *Lactobacillus bulgaricus* and *Streptococcus thermophilus*. It has the same amount of milk fat as the milk it was made from.

Greek yogurt is more creamy and dense in texture and flavor than ordinary yogurt.

Crème fraîche is a cultured cream with a tart, tangy flavor, which is very popular in Europe.

Sour cream, made by adding a culture to pasteurized homogenized cream, has a butter content that is not less than 18 percent and it is used as a condiment or in baked goods.

Buttermilk has a tart flavor and thick texture, produced by adding a culture to fresh, pasteurized, skim, or low-fat milk.

Storage

Fresh dairy products should be kept below 41°F (5°C) in a refrigerator. It is important to keep them away from other food items, such as onions or garlic, as they will absorb strong odors and flavors. It's important to keep containers tightly closed and to use the products by their sell-by date.

Cheese

Cheese is one of the oldest, most widely used processed foods. It can be served alone at the cheese course or as a principal ingredient in, or an accompaniment to, numerous dishes–from breakfast and main courses to snacks and desserts.

For centuries natural cheeses have been made using cow's, goat's, or sheep's milk. Casein or milk proteins are coagulated by adding rennet. The milk separates into solid curds and liquid whey. The curds can be made into fresh cheese, such as ricotta (see Workout 149). Further processing, by cutting, kneading, and cooking, makes "green cheese," which is molded and drained. Seasoning and bacteria may be added to develop flavor, color, texture, and age.

Some cheeses have a natural rind, while others may be wax-coated. Fresh cheeses don't have rind. The higher the moisture content, the more perishable it will be. Hard cheeses have low moisture and will last several weeks, or longer, while soft cheeses deteriorate quickly. Fat content can range from as low as 20 percent to triple cream, which is at least 60 percent.

Fresh, unripened cheese

This is referred to as "fromage blanc" or "fromage frais." With average moisture content of 40-80 percent, this type is mild and creamy,

149 Workout: Making ricotta

Ricotta is very easy to make and tastes wonderfully sweet and milky. Remember that this is a fresh cheese, high in moisture, and it needs to be refrigerated at all times.

Recipe
- 1 qt (946 ml) whole milk
- 3 fl oz (90 ml) fresh lime juice

Allow the milk to come to room temperature, then pour into a saucepan and slowly heat to 180°F (82°C). Keep the milk at that temperature for five minutes. Remove from the heat and add the lime juice, stirring continuously until curds start to form. Gently pour the curds into a china cup lined with muslin and discard the whey (liquid). Allow the cheese to rest for one hour. Tie the four corners of the muslin together to make a bag and suspend it in a tall, covered container overnight in the refrigerator. Unwrap the cheese and season with salt. Use the cheese as you would commercially produced ricotta.

Types of cheese

Name	Type	Milk	Characteristic	% fat	Culinary use
Asiago	hard	cow	light yellow, mild to sharp	30	salads, pasta, fruit, bread
Boursin	soft, triple cream	cow	rindless, smooth, creamy, soft	75	table, chicken dishes
Camembert	soft	cow, goat	soft, light, yellow, mild, edible rind	45	table, sandwiches
Cheddar	firm	cow	light to medium, mild to sharp	45-50	table, sandwiches, melting
Fontina	semi-soft	cow, sheep	medium, yellow, mild to grassy	45	table, fondues, sandwiches
Gorgonzola	semi-soft	cow, goat	medium, yellow, marbling, tangy	48	table, salads, pizza
Gruyère	firm	cow	flat, beige wheel, brown rind, fruity	45-50	fondues, gratins, soups
Manchego	firm	sheep	white to yellowish, sharp, nutty	45-57	table, salads
Marscapone	fresh	cow	soft, pale yellow, buttery	70-75	tiramisu, fruit
Mozzerella	fresh	buffalo	soft, white, tender, maybe smoked	40-45	pizza, Caprese salad
Parmesan	hard	cow	straw-colored, sharp, nutty, salty	32-35	pasta, risotto, salads
Pecorino Romano	hard	sheep	white, black rind, salty, peppery	35	table, pasta, salads Queso
Provolone	firm	cow	pale yellow to brown, oily, smoked	45	table, bread, cold meats
Qaxaca	fresh	cow	semi-soft, white, stretched curd	45	quesadillas, nachos, tacos
Ricotta	fresh	cow	soft, moist, white, grainy	4-10	cheesecake, pastry filling
Roquefort	semi-soft	sheep	blue-veined, deep flavor, spicy	45	table, salads
Taleggio	semi-soft	cow	light, yellow, salty, strong	48	table, salads, cooking

with a tart tanginess. Cream cheese is made from cow's milk in the United States and has a 35 percent fat content. Feta, a fresh cheese from Greece, is made from goat's or sheep's milk. It is white and flaky and is pickled in brine.

Soft cheese

High in moisture, creamy, and delicious, soft cheeses are among the most popular cheeses around the world. A well-known example is Brie, from France. It contains 60 percent fat and is made into round, flat disks. It is best when it oozes out of the rind. Buy it when the cheese is bulging; if it is hard and firm it has not ripened yet. It is best served after dinner.

Semi-soft, firm, and hard

Dating back to the Middle Ages, these cheeses are sometimes referred to as "monastery," or "Trappist," cheeses. Without being too hard or too brittle, firm cheese has a close texture and is flaky. Cheddar is mostly produced in the United Kingdom, North America, and Australia. Flavors range from mild to very sharp, depending on age. Hard cheeses are composed of about 30 percent moisture and are carefully aged. They are often grated for use.

Processed cheese

This cheese is manufactured by grinding up one or more natural cheeses, heating, and blending them with emulsifiers and other ingredients, and then pouring into molds to harden. It is very cheap to buy and lasts a long time. It melts easily and because of its blandness it appeals to those who don't like strong cheese.

Storage and serving

Most cheeses can be stored in the refrigerator, if they are well wrapped. Firm to hard cheese will last for weeks, while fresh cheese tends to spoil in seven to ten days because of its high moisture content. The most important rule concerning cheese is to serve it at room temperature. Only then will the true, full flavor develop. It is best to cut it just before serving.

---

150 **Workout:** Making Parmesan wafers

Parmesan wafers make a great snack, or they can be used with a cheese plate and served with freshly made ricotta or mozzarella, tomatoes, basil, and a balsamic vinegar dressing. This dish works best if you use the freshly grated rather than the ready-grated variety.

1 Finely grate the cheese, take a nonstick sheet pan and use a 2-in (5-cm) cookie cutter as a template and fill with the cheese.

2 Place the sheet pan in the oven, set at 355ºF (180ºC), for eight to ten minutes. Remove as soon as the cheese melts and fuses.

3 Allow the wafers to cool slightly on the sheet pan, then remove to a wire rack to cool completely. The wafers can be stored for three to four days in an airtight container.

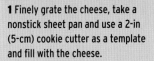

1

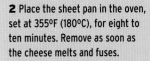

2

3

---

151 **Workout:** Taste-test your local cheeses

Artisan, or artisanal, cheese is cheese that is produced by hand in small batches by cheese enthusiasts, and sold especially at farmers' markets. Particular attention is paid to the tradition of the craft of cheese-making, using only the very best ingredients. Buying these cheeses is a great way to support your local farmers' market and also educate your palate at the same time. Try buying a different cheese each week, ask the maker about the ingredients and how the cheese was made. Also find out if you can cook with it and what it is best served with. But most of all, taste it and enjoy it. You can only become a great chef if you have great taste buds.

Cooking with cheese

The three most widely used cheeses to cook with are: Cheddar, Swiss-type, and Parmesan, which are used in soups, sauces, soufflés, and hot and cold sandwiches.

Cooking tips:
1 Too high a heat and the cheese will toughen because of the high amount of protein. Use a low heat and if you are using cheese in a sauce never boil it.
2 If you are melting cheese, grate it first. This will allow it to melt uniformly.
3 Aged cheese melts and blends into food more easily than young cheese.
4 Strong, aged cheese adds more flavor to food than mild, young cheese.

Eggs

Eggs, particularly chicken's eggs, are an excellent food for humans, because they are high in protein, low in cost, and readily available anywhere: at the farmers' market, grocery store, even the gas station. Eggs can be served at virtually any meal; they can be cooked in the shell to soft, medium, or hard, poached, fried, scrambled, or prepared as omelets or soufflés. As simple as eggs seem, to become a great chef you must master the techniques of cooking them to perfection.

Modern egg sizes

Size	Mass per egg
Jumbo	greater than 2.5 oz (71 g)
Very large/extra large	greater than 2.25 oz (64 g)
Large	greater than 2 oz (57 g)
Medium	greater than 1.75 oz (50 g)
Small	greater than 1.5 oz (43 g)
Peewee	greater than 1.25 oz (35 g)

Nutritional value

Eggs provide the body with vitamins A, D, K, and the B-complex vitamins. Recent research suggests that eggs are not as bad for the heart as was once thought; four a week are now suggested by most authorities as acceptable as part of a balanced diet.

The makeup of an egg

There are three main parts to an egg: shell, yolk, and albumen. The shell is made of calcium carbonate, and the breed of hen determines its color, ranging from palest white to rich, dark brown. Brown eggs are often thought to be "better," but the shell has no effect on flavor, nutrition, or quality. The shell is porous, so store eggs away from strong-smelling foods. The yolk is the yellow part of the egg and usually makes up one-third of volume. It contains most of the egg's fat, vitamins, and minerals, too. Lecithin is also contained in the yolk, and it is this substance that binds sauces. The albumen of the egg is referred to as the "white" and constitutes two-thirds of the volume and contains more than half of its protein and riboflavin. Egg whites coagulate between 144°F and 149°F (62°C–65°C), while the yolk coagulates between 149°F and 195°F (65°C–70°C).

Egg grading

Eggs are graded according to interior quality and the condition and appearance of the shell. Eggs of any quality grade may differ in weight.
Grade AA eggs have whites that are thick and firm; yolks that are high, round, and free from defects; and clean, unbroken shells. Grades AA and A are best for frying and poaching.
Grade A eggs have the characteristics of Grade AA eggs, except that the whites are "reasonably" firm. This is the quality most often sold in stores.
Grade B eggs have whites that are sometimes thinner and yolks that may be wider and flatter than eggs of higher grades. The shells must be unbroken, but may show slight stains. This quality is seldom found in retail stores because such eggs are usually used to make liquid, frozen, and dried-egg products, as well as other products that contain eggs.

Chicken eggs are graded by size for the purpose of sales. The United States Department of Agriculture sizing is based by weight per dozen. The most common size of chicken egg is "large" and is the egg size that is commonly required in recipes.

Practicing basic techniques
The three basic techniques that any chef will need to know about eggs are boiling, poaching, and frying. Practice makes perfect, so practice as much as you can. Eggs are easy to obtain and inexpensive to buy and make a great meal at any time of the day.

152 Workout: Boiling eggs

Take a medium-sized saucepan and fill with enough water to cover the eggs. Remove from the refrigerator and let them come to room temperature. Bring the water to a boil and slide the eggs into the pan. Bring the water back to a simmer and start your timer. Depending on egg size three to five minutes will soft-boil, five to seven minutes will medium-boil, and ten to twelve minutes will hard-boil.

153 Workout: Scrambled eggs

Making scrambled eggs takes time to perfect, but the good news is that every time you practice, you, your family, or friends get to eat the finished result. Scrambled eggs are great on their own or served with smoked salmon or chopped chives. For a touch of luxury, they are also truly amazing served with freshly sliced truffles.

1 Whisk two to three eggs per portion and add a small amount of cream. Whisk until they are thoroughly blended.

2 Over medium heat, melt a small amount of butter and add the whisked eggs. Stir continuously; season as the eggs start to cook.

3 Remove from the heat just as the eggs start to set—they should be soft, creamy, and runny, not overcooked.

154 Workout: Fried egg

Heat a small amount of oil in a pan until it begins to sizzle. Crack open the egg and gently drop it into the hot oil. Fry for one to two minutes, basting with the oil. The white will firm up and the edges should start to crisp, but the yolk should remain soft. For over-easy style flip with a spatula and cook for a further 15 seconds.

155 Workout: Poaching an egg

Bring a large saucepan of water to simmering point. Add a small amount of vinegar to the water to help the protein in the egg to set. Break the egg into a cup; this will make it easier to drop the egg into the water. Using a whisk, make a vortex in the center of the water and drop the egg into it. Bring the water back to the simmering point and time the egg for three to four minutes. The white should be set and the yolk still runny.

Eggs on the menu

If you apply for a position in the kitchen of a large hotel, breakfast chef is one of the first positions you will probably be offered. Now that you are familiar with the basic skills involved in cooking eggs, you need to concentrate on speed, timing, and precision. Eggs are used throughout the menu, in many different dishes. You will need to practice how to separate eggs, how to whip up egg whites, and also how to make crêpes.

Cooking methods

Boiled eggs are cooked in their shells to hard, soft, or coddled. They are served in their shells, or with their shells removed and used in other preparations, such as deviled eggs (see Workout 156). It is best to boil them in simmering rather than fast-boiling water, in a large pot, with enough water to completely cover them. Start timing your eggs from the moment the water returns to a simmer after you have placed the eggs in the pot. If you overcook eggs you will notice that a a green ring appears around the yolk. This is a chemical reaction between iron and sulfur, which is naturally present in the egg.

Poached eggs. When poaching eggs you slip fresh, shelled eggs into simmering water in a large pan and gently cook them until the egg holds its shape. The fresher the egg, the less likely the white will be to spread. You can serve poached eggs as eggs Benedict (poached eggs, English muffin, bacon, and hollandaise sauce) or on top of hash browns or as a garnish to a hearty soup. Added vinegar to the simmering water encourages the egg protein to set faster. You can cook poached eggs in advance by slightly undercooking them, then shocking them in cold water to stop the cooking process. You then trim

them to obtain an even shape, hold them in cold water, and when you need them reheat them in simmering water before serving.

Fried eggs are cooked in a pan or on a griddle with hot oil or clarified butter. It's important to use the freshest eggs available to produce a perfect fried egg, sunny side up or over (turned once).

Scrambled eggs. Use a pan or a griddle with a small amount of oil or clarified butter. Choose really fresh eggs whisked with a small amount of milk or cream. There are two scrambling methods: either stir the eggs constantly over low heat to obtain a delicate curd and creamy texture, or stir them less often to produce a large curd and a firmer texture. Season after cooking has started, garnish with fresh herbs, cheese, smoked salmon, or truffles.

Omelets. When you are making omelets, you will get the best results by using an omelet pan that has been well seasoned or is nonstick. It is best to keep omelet pans for just making

Storage

Eggs need to be stored at a temperature below 45°F (7°C) and at a relative humidity of 70 to 80 percent. When making poached or fried eggs try to use eggs that are as fresh as possible; you can use older eggs for boiling or for making meringues. The older an egg is the thinner the white will become. An egg will age more in one day if left out of the refrigerator than an egg that is left in the refrigerator for over a week. Rotate eggs as they come in and do not use them if they are cracked or dirty. Store eggs away from strongly flavored foods, to reduce odor absorption.

156 Workout: Making deviled eggs

Boil the eggs, then cool them down, take off the shell and cut them in half lengthwise, remove the yolks, mash with a fork, and add mayonnaise, dry mustard, Worcestershire sauce, and seasoning. Mix these together until you have a smooth paste. Place the mixture into a piping bag with a star tube/tip and pipe it into each white half. Finally, decorate with chopped parsley, dill, capers, sliced olives, paprika, or red or black caviar.

Batter

Batters are a mixture of flour, liquid, and eggs and sometimes you can add cream or even beer. They can be sweet for pancakes and maple syrup, or savory, as in the great British classic, Yorkshire pudding.

omelets, and nothing else, to avoid scratching them. Use a wooden spoon or spatula to stir the eggs as they cook. This will also reduce the possibility of scratching. Omelets start out as scrambled eggs, but once they start to set are usually folded or rolled over. Frittatas (Italian) or tortillas (Spanish), or farmer-style omelets are also known as "flat" omelets, which are finished by cooking in the oven. You can garnish or fill omelets with sautéed vegetables, cheese, steamed potatoes, and smoked fish.

Soufflés. Two things make a good savory soufflé: a base, which is usually made from thick béchamel, and whisked egg whites. You can flavor the base with grated cheese, spinach, or possibly even shellfish.

157 Workout: Making crêpes

Crêpes, or pancakes, are very popular and easy to make, and can be served savory or sweet, depending on the filling. Start by sifting the flour, salt, and sugar into a large bowl, then whisk in the eggs to form a smooth batter the consistency of heavy cream.

1 Melt the butter in a saucepan carefully, trying not to burn it. Then pour into the batter mixture.

2 Place a knob of butter into the crêpe pan. As soon as it melts, pour in a ladle of batter and spread it evenly across the pan.

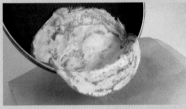

3 Cook for about 45–60 seconds, then shake the pan to make sure it is moving around. Toss the pancake or use your spatula to turn it over.

4 Cook for a further 30–45 seconds before turning out. Serve immediately or place on wax paper, allow to cool, and refrigerate for later.

158 Workout: Separating eggs

Crack open the shell on a flat surface and then carefully open the shell with your fingers. Pour the yolk from one shell to the other, allowing the white to dribble into the bowl underneath. You should end up with one bowl of yolks and another of whites.

159 Workout: Whisking egg whites

Whisked egg whites are used in a variety of dishes, such as meringues, soufflés, and mousses. Start by separating the yolks from the whites and placing the whites in a grease-free bowl. You can add a touch of cream of tartar to help stiffen them.

1 Using either a balloon whisk or an electric whisk, beat the egg whites until they become foamy.

2 At this stage you need to add about two-thirds of the sugar to the egg whites. Continue to beat until stiff and glossy.

3 Carefully sprinkle the remainder of the sugar over the egg whites and gently fold into the meringue mix with a metal spoon.

Baking

Baking and pastry is an art in itself, and a chef needs a basic understanding of how baking ingredients work together.

Meringues, formed when egg whites and sugar are whipped, can be used to make soufflés, icing for cakes, or be slow-dried to become crisp shells that you can fill with fruit, ice cream, or mousse. Learn why chocolate, once the delicacy of kings, evolved into everyone's favorite treat. From a sacred and revered health food to a modern scientific wonder, chocolate is now one of the chef's great ingredients and is used to make the most indulgent and delicious of dishes.

Sandwiches, composed of great bread, a spread, and a fantastic filling, provide a wonderful array of snack options for your customers. Find out how an imaginative choice of ingredients and creative presentation can provide an attractive and appetizing light meal.

Sandwiches

Sandwiches can give the chef an almost endless choice to offer customers, and they find their way onto most menus, from elegant receptions and afternoon teas to substantial but casual appetizers and entrées.

Sandwich types

• Hot sandwiches include hot dogs, hamburgers, tacos, quesadillas, burritos, and wraps, which can be grilled or deep-fried.
• Hot, open-faced sandwiches are made with bread that has been toasted, grilled, or left fresh, on a plate with the filling piled high and eaten with a knife and fork. Pizza is often placed in this category.
• Cold sandwiches may be "open" or "closed." They are not supposed to be served hot, so you should use precooked meats, fish, or shellfish with ready-prepared vegetables and spreads that have been chilled before use. A basic sandwich uses two slices of bread, whereas a multi-decker sandwich could be made with three, or more, slices.
• Tea sandwiches are normally small, fancy-trimmed breads that have been cut into diamonds, circles, or pinwheels, and are served at receptions or for afternoon tea.
• Cold open-faced sandwiches include the popular open-faced Scandinavian sandwich, known as smørbrød. Presentation is most important, to give the sandwich the best visual appeal possible, since everything is on show to the customer.

The term "sandwich" came into use 200 years ago with the fourth Earl of Sandwich, Sir John Montague, who used to like to eat meat and cheese between two slices of bread while playing card games. A sandwich is often one of the first things people learn to make in their kitchen. Even if they claim not to be able to cook, almost anyone can make a delicious sandwich using leftovers from the fridge.

One of my first creations as "chef to be" was in my mother's kitchen, making a fresh lettuce sandwich. The lettuce was picked from my father's garden, washed, dried, with a little spread of mayonnaise, on two slices of whole wheat bread and a sprinkle of salt. To this day, I still can remember how delicious that sandwich tasted and it is an inspiring memory.

Most restaurants these days, no matter how big or small, from mom-and-pop restaurants to the Dorchester in London, include a range of sandwiches on their menus. They are quick and easy to produce and lend themselves to a chef's creativity and imagination. When you serve the best bread with an amazing filling, you can keep lunchtime customers coming back for more, day in, day out.

Sandwiches are composed of only three basic elements: great bread, a spread, and a fantastic filling, and you can always finish off your presentation with a garnish on the side.

Bread

The choice of breads is endless, from sliced white and wheat loaves to uncut, rolls, biscuits, croissants, bagels, whole wheat breads, fruit and nut breads, to wraps, flat breads, pocket breads such as pita, and flavorful breads such as Italian foccacia. All make great breads to hold the spread and filling, giving the sandwich shape and making it easy to handle and eat. Bread adds color, flavor, texture, and nutrition and also gives whatever filling you use a different appearance, depending on what bread you decide on. Remember the number-one rule: make sure that the bread is fresh. There is nothing worse than biting into a stale piece of bread, no matter how good the filling is. Also make sure that the bread does not overpower the filling and that it is firm enough to withstand the spread and filling without becoming soggy or breaking up when you try and take a bite.

Spread

The main purpose of a spread is to prevent the moisture from reaching the filling and soaking into the bread, at the same time adding moisture, flavor, and richness to the sandwich. Butter is a popular spread; it acts as an excellent moisture barrier, while adding flavor and richness. Compound butter or flavored butters also add another dimension rather than just

 Workout: Sandwich station setup

Have everything ready ahead of time, so you can quickly and efficiently assemble your sandwiches without moving about the kitchen. Mix your fillings, wash and dry vegetables, such as lettuce, prepare spreads and dressings, slice meats and cheeses, slice tomatoes and cucumbers, and prepare garnishes. Have your bread chosen and stacked, equipment cleaned, ready at hand. This creates a good *mise en place*.

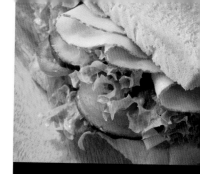

using plain butter. Mayonnaise, on the other hand, is probably the number-one spread; it complements almost every filling, from poultry to eggs and cheese. Just like butter, you can add flavorings such as curry powder, mustard, or even fresh pesto. Other spreads could include tapenades, hummus, spreadable cheeses such as ricotta, cream cheese, mascarpone, or crème fraîche to puréed vegetables such as roasted red peppers, avocado pulp, or guacamole.

Filling

Popular fillings include beef, chicken, turkey, pork, fish, and shellfish to roasted vegetables, eggs, and cheese. Whatever you choose, make sure, if the sandwich is cold, that all the ingredients are served cold, using precooked meats that have been properly chilled. Some hot sandwich fillings may be cooked to order. Again, just make sure, like the bread, that all filling ingredients are fresh. If you are using lettuce, make sure that it is really crisp. The filling is the body of the sandwich; this is really what your customer is paying for, so make sure it is good.

Garnishing sandwiches

Most sandwiches are cut into halves, thirds, or quarters, making them easy to eat. This also adds to the presentation by showing off the filling's colors and textures and adding height to the plate. Suggested garnishes are sliced tomatoes, onion rings, pickles, potato chips, or French fries—all popular—to carved vegetables, dips, spreads, relishes, fruit, and olives.

161 Workout: Making shaped sandwiches

Make a variety of sandwiches of different shapes and sizes, using different breads and a variety of spreads and fillings. Try using cookie cutters to create more interesting circular shapes—you can even experiment with heart-shaped cutters! Try your ideas out on your friends and family.

162 Workout: Making a wrap

Wraps have all the handheld, utensil-free convenience of a sandwich, while offering the chance to cross culinary borders with new flavor combinations—anything from Mexico's tacos, France's crêpes, Vietnam's spring rolls, the Middle East's stuffed pita, Greece's gyros, to China's moo shu. They can be tortilla made with flour or corn, whole wheat flavored with pesto, jalapeño, lemon, spinach, or tomato. Or you could use pita bread, naan, spring rolls, or crêpes.

1 Spread the wrap bread with mayonnaise, butter, hummus, or pesto.

2 Place the meats and vegetables across one side of the tortilla.

3 Now tightly roll the tortilla around the filling. You can roll the wrap in plastic wrap to hold its shape and refrigerate.

Pastry, doughs, & cake batters

At their most basic, pastry goods are shells, cases, and containers for fillings, but with practice a skilled chef can turn these simple flour and water items into unique works of art.

The ever-tempting croissant
Did you know that the classic French breakfast pastry, the croissant, originated in Budapest, Hungary, to celebrate the city's liberation from Turkey in 1686? The crescent shape came from the crescent moon of the Turkish national flag.

There is no mystery to making a perfect pastry dough or cake mix, yet many chefs are apprehensive about tackling them. Almost all pastry dough or cake mixes are made up of four main ingredients: flour, water, fat, and salt. Occasionally butter and eggs are added to the dough to add richness and texture.

Rubbed-in pastry doughs

This type of pastry is made with all-purpose flour, which you should weigh out carefully, along with any leavener. You then sift the mixture to blend the flour and leavener and also sift other dry ingredients, such as salt or spices, along with the flour, so that all dry ingredients are equally distributed. The most common fats used for this mixing method are butter, shortening, and lard, or a possible combination of two or three of them. The fats need to be very cold and cut into cubes, then added to the dry ingredients and rubbed in. The palms of your hands will warm the dough, so use just your fingertips and lightly rub the mixture together. The larger the flakes of fat the "flakier" the finished product. This dough is referred to as a "flaky" dough, which is best suited for pies and tarts, filled with a sweet or savory filling, and then baked. If you rub the fat further into the dry ingredients to resemble breadcrumbs, this is referred to as a "mealy" dough and is good for making blind-baked shells to be filled with custard or lemon filling before being re-baked until the filling sets. Once you have decided on a flaky or mealy dough, it's time to mix in any liquid that the recipe asks for. This should be just enough for the moisture to bring the ingredients together. At this stage, wrap the dough in plastic wrap and chill it in the refrigerator before rolling out and using it to make biscuits, scones, soda breads, or pies.

Creamed cake batters

Make sure all your ingredients are at room temperature before you start. Place the butter or shortening and sugar into a mixing bowl and beat them together until they are smooth, light, and creamy. The creaminess is created when you beat the granules of sugar into the fat, causing it to aerate. Add the beaten eggs and sifted dry ingredients gradually, depending on the amount of flour and liquid, which you may have to add in two or three stages. Always start and end with the flour. You can also add other flavorings, such as vanilla or chocolate extracts, at this stage. Lightly grease and flour the baking pans and then pour in the batter. You can use the creaming method for muffins, cakes, quick breads, and cookies.

163 Workout: How to make shortcrust pastry

Shortcrust pastry is so easy to make and very versatile to use. Make sure you weigh out all your ingredients carefully. Once made, allow the pastry to rest for 30 minutes before rolling out and using. The simple formula is half as much fat (butter or lard) as flour, plus a little water.

1 Sift the flour and salt into a large bowl. Using your fingertips rub in the lard or butter.

2 Rub the dry ingredients together until the mixture resembles breadcrumbs. Then add 2 tsp of water and gently knead to a dough.

164 Workout: Blind baking

Pastry cases for tarts often need to be cooked before the filling is added. Grease and line the tart mold with your pastry, then place a sheet of parchment paper over the pastry and fill with dried beans or rice. This will stop the pastry from bubbling or buckling while being baked. Once baked, remove the parchment paper and beans, cool, and fill with your filling. This is known as blind baking.

165 Workout: Making puff pastry

Sift 8 oz (240 g) flour and salt, rub in 1 oz (30 g) lard, add 8 fl oz (240 ml) cold water. Mix to a dough and knead. Wrap and allow to rest for 30 minutes. Roll out to a rectangle of 5 x 10 in (13 x 25 cm). Roll the middle third of the pastry a little wider to create what looks like two wings on the side of the pastry.

1 Flour 6 oz (150 g) butter lightly and roll out to 4 x 3 in (10 x 8 cm). Place the butter on the pastry and fold over the wings. Fold over the top.

2 Fold over the bottom of the pastry to form a parcel. Then turn the parcel 90 degrees so that the folded edges face you.

3 Carefully flatten the pastry-covered butter with the rolling pin.

4 Roll out the pastry to the original rectangle shape you started with.

5 Take your time and fold it into three again. Fold the nearest side to you into the middle, then fold over the other side again, forming a parcel.

6 Turn the pastry 90 degrees again, so that the folded edges face you. Allow to rest for 30 minutes, then repeat three more times.

Foamed batter

There are three types of foaming method. "Cold foam" is when whole eggs are whipped with the sugar into a batter. The "warm" method is when you whisk it over a heated water bath. This method makes a more stable foam as the eggs are partially cooked. The "separated" method is where you separate yolks from whites and whip them separately to gain maximum aeration. At this stage, whichever method you use, add dry ingredients, which you should fold in carefully to retain as much air as possible. You can use this batter to make angel food cake and chiffon cake.

Choux pastry

Choux pastry is used to make cream puffs, éclairs, Spanish churros, choux swans, or savory gougers. As the batter expands from the steam inside the baking dough, it forms a hollow shell, which, when cooled, can be filled with cream or pastry cream. Literally translated, pâté á choux means "cabbage paste," a reference to the cabbage-like shape of cream puffs. It is made by adding the flour to the warmed liquid and melted butter before adding beaten eggs.

Take a pan that is large enough to mix all ingredients together. Melt the butter and liquid in the pan. When it starts to boil, add the sifted, dry ingredients in one amount. Stir vigorously, until the dough starts to pull away from the sides of the pan, forming a ball. Transfer the mixture to a mixing bowl and allow it to cool slightly. Gradually pour in the beaten eggs in three or four additions, working the dough until smooth.

Laminated dough

Puff pastry is the principal example of this kind of dough, in which fat is rolled into a previously made dough, which when cooked allows steam to expand in the space between the layers of pastry. This gives a crisp, light, flaky product used for turnovers, croissants, and Danish pastries.

Baking, cooling, and storing

Follow your chosen recipe for oven temperatures and baking times; they will vary, depending on what you are making. To cool, most items are placed on a cooling wire, so that cold air can circulate around the product. Most cakes are allowed to cool slightly before being turned out, whereas most pie cases are allowed to cool in the mold before being removed.

The shelflife of most pastry goods is short if left exposed to air. Once chilled, pastries should be wrapped or kept in an airtight container. They can be frozen when they are tightly wrapped in plastic wrap. Before serving or using they should be allowed to thaw at room temperature.

Profiteroles
The crisp, golden-brown light pastry of the ever-popular profiterole, filled with chantilly cream and smothered in rich, dark chocolate sauce. What more could your customers want?

Meringues & chocolate

Two basic ingredients, egg whites and sugar, can form the most delicious dish—meringues. You can use them to make soufflés, cake icing, or fill them with fruit or cream. From a delicacy for kings to everyone's favorite treat, chocolate is one of the chef's great ingredients; a most indulgent dish.

"Meringue" refers to egg whites and sugar whipped to a hard or soft texture, depending on the ratio of sugar to eggs. A low sugar ratio will produce a soft meringue to fold into a mousse or soufflé, while a higher sugar ratio will produce a hard meringue for buttercream or baked Alaska. You can also caramelize it under the broiler or create disks of baked meringue to make a layered cake filled with fresh fruit and cream.

Meringue science

Egg whites are made up of 85 percent water and protein, and it is this protein, when whipped, that traps air bubbles. This stabilizes the protein to make foam. When the foam is heated the air expands, the water evaporates, and the protein coagulates, preventing the collapse of the foam structure. The best type of bowl for whipping egg whites is the copper or stainless-steel variety. When adding the sugar, add it in a steady stream as the eggs start to increase in volume. The sugar, like the protein, stabilizes the foam and creates a smooth, silky texture.

Meringue types

Common/French meringues are also known as "cold" meringues; they don't need to be baked and you can use them in chocolate mousse or soufflés. Whip the egg whites briskly until they triple in volume. Then reduce speed to medium and slowly add the sugar to obtain a light, fluffy foam. Use it immediately to make rings, shells, or in sponge cakes or soufflés.

Swiss meringues are made by adding sugar and whites in a bowl over a hot-water bath. Whisk until the mixture has reached a temperature of 115°F-165°F (46°C-74°C). Then whisk at medium speed, until the mixture thickens and cools. Use it to lighten mousses and creams and make fillings for cakes or buttercream.

Italian meringues are a combination of simple syrup (water and sugar boiled together) and common/French meringue. To prepare the syrup boil the sugar and water to 230°F-250°F (110°C-121°C). While boiling, make the common/French meringue, reduce the speed to medium, and slowly pour in the hot simple syrup. Continue until the meringue thickens and cools. Use Italian meringues to decorate cakes and lighten batters.

Low fat

Meringues are naturally low in fat so they are ideal to use as a substitute for fatty pastries when making desserts. You can use them for pie toppings and fillings, especially when flavored with vanilla, cocoa powder, or ground nuts. They are also gluten-free and can be used to make shells filled with fruit or baked hard and served as cookies.

166 Workout: Piping a meringue

This works well with a Swiss meringue mixture. Place a piping tube in the piping bag and fill with meringue. Do not overfill. Apply an even pressure with the palm of your hand and carefully pipe the desired shape.

1 Take a sheet pan and line it with wax paper, place a plate on the paper and draw around it with a pencil. Turn over the paper and use the circle to pipe the meringue around.

2 Pipe more rings on top, then pipe the sides from the bottom to the top of the nest.

3 Try piping scrolls, shells, or rosettes along the top edge. Bake in the oven on a low setting until crisp.

167 Workout: Making a perfect meringue

Use a hand balloon whisk in a copper or stainless-steel bowl rather than an electric mixer to get an even-textured meringue. Use 2 oz (60 g) superfine sugar to each egg white.

Recipe
• 4 large eggs
• 8 oz (240 g) sugar

1 Carefully separate the whites from the yolks. Place the whites in the bowl and gently beat them together.

2 Increase the beating speed, until you have achieved a soft-peak consistency.

3 Gradually add the sugar and beat until the consistency has changed to a hard peak.
4 If you can turn the bowl upside down without the meringue falling out, you have achieved the desired consistency.

Chocolate

Chocolate comes from the berries of the cacao tree, which grows in Mexico, Ecuador, Brazil, and in some parts of Africa.

Couverture chocolate

Couverture (koo-vehr-TYOOR) is the French word for "coating." It is high-quality dark, milk, or white chocolate containing at least 32 percent cocoa butter, used to coat candies or other products. It must be tempered before being used to give a thin coating to confections and pastries.

Compound chocolate

This is also called "coating," but is made from hydrogenated fat and lecithin, not cocoa butter. This means that it need not be tempered before being used for coating, dipping, or molding.

Dark and milk chocolate

Dark, or pure, chocolate is marketed as unsweetened chocolate and referred to as "baking" or "bitter" chocolate. It requires between 50 and 58 percent cocoa butter, with no added sugar or milk solids, giving it a bitter taste. Dark chocolate is used for cake fillings and mousses. Milk chocolate is the favorite eating chocolate and is made from cocoa paste that has been finely conched and combined with cocoa butter, sugar, and vanilla. Milk chocolate must contain at least 12 percent milk solids and 10 percent chocolate liquor. It is used for confections, glazes, mousses, candies, and as a coating chocolate. Do not substitute milk chocolate for dark chocolate in any product that must be baked, as the milk solids tend to burn.

White chocolate

This is not really a chocolate, but is made with sugar, cocoa butter, lecithin, vanilla, and dried or condensed milk and is used in confectionery.

Cocoa powder

Cocoa powder is the brown, dry powder that remains after the cocoa butter has been removed from the chocolate liquor. Ordinary cocoa has no added sweeteners or flavorings and can be used in baked products.

Storage of chocolate

Store chocolate, well wrapped, away from strong odors and moisture in a cool, dry, ventilated area. Chocolate should not be stored in a refrigerator because this can cause moisture, called "sugar bloom," to gather on the surface, which will result in a gritty texture if it is melted. Sometimes the bloom shows as a white deposit on the surface. This merely indicates that the chocolate has been stored above 21ºC (70ºF) and some of the cocoa butter has melted and then recrystallized on the surface. It can still be used without problems when tempered.

Cocoa powder can be stored in tightly sealed containers in a cool, dry area for up to a year without loss of flavor.

Favorite snack
Known as "food of the gods," chocolate is considered to be an extraordinary food and is the favorite snack of many.

168 Workout: Tempering chocolate

Tempering is a process of heating and cooking the chocolate slowly to stabilize the emulsified cocoa solids and cocoa fat.

1 Melt the chocolate over a double boiler to a temperature of 110ºF (43ºC). Pour about half of the melted chocolate onto a marble tabletop.
2 Use a palette knife and work the chocolate back and forth with the knife for about three to four minutes, until the chocolate is silky smooth.

3 Scrape the chocolate back into the bowl and blend. The temperature should be around 85ºF (29ºC). The chocolate is tempered and ready for use.

169 Workout: Chocolate mousse

Few desserts are as popular as chocolate mousse. Try this easy recipe.

Recipe (yield: serves 4)
• 8 oz (240 g) dark chocolate
• 4 oz (120 g) unsalted butter
• 3 egg yolks
• 5 egg whites
• 1 oz (30 g) sugar
• 4 fl oz (120 ml) heavy cream

1 Melt the chocolate and butter in a double boiler over low heat.
2 Whisk in the egg yolks one at a time. In a separate bowl, whip the egg whites until they reach stiff peak stage. Then fold in the sugar.
3 Using a spatula, fold the whipped egg whites into the chocolate mixture and remove from the heat.

4 Whip the cream to soft-peak stage, slightly cool the mousse mixture. Then fold in the cream.
5 Chill the mousse, then place it into a piping bag and pipe into molds, garnish with berries, shaved chocolate, or mint leaves.

Custards & creamed desserts

The simple combination of cream, eggs, and milk gives a silky smooth and eminently satisfying dessert, or the starting point for numerous fillings, creams, mousses, and ice creams.

Almost all creams and custards are cooked, but they can be served either warm or cold. You, as a chef, must learn how to master the heating of the milk and eggs; too much heat and the eggs become lumpy; too cold and the mixture will not thicken to hold the moisture of the dessert.

Custard

A custard is a liquid that has been thickened with eggs. As the eggs heat up, the protein coagulates and thickens the liquid; the consistency of the sauce depends on how many eggs you have used, whether they are whole or just the yolks, or if you have used milk or cream. The more eggs you use, the thicker and richer the sauce will be. The same theory applies if you use cream instead of milk.

Vanilla custard sauce

Vanilla custard sauce (crème anglaise) is made with egg yolks, sugar, and milk. You can use cream for a thicker, richer sauce, or try half-and-half. This is usually flavored with vanilla bean or pure vanilla extract. When making custard you have to be careful not to allow the sauce to boil, otherwise the eggs will curdle. You also need to stir the sauce constantly otherwise it will burn onto the pan, giving the sauce a burnt flavor.

Use a thermometer to monitor the temperature and do not allow the sauce to exceed 190°F (88°C). The ideal temperature is 185°F (85°C) and should be just enough to thicken the sauce and coat the back of a spoon. You can serve custard hot or cold with fruit or pastries, or you can use it as a base for ice cream. If you make a thick version you can use it to make a classic English sherry trifle. Alternatively, pour it into a ramekin and bake it in a water bath in the oven, at a temperature not exceeding 212°F (100°C). Then allow it to cool, sprinkle with sugar, and caramelize it with a blow torch to make classic French crème brulée. Baked custards, properly baked, have a smooth texture that is firm enough to slice, like crème caramel or a flan. Add other ingredients and you have the base for cheesecake, rice pudding, and bread pudding.

Pastry cream

Pastry cream (crème pâtissière) is made just like vanilla custard sauce, only it is thickened with a starch, such as flour, cornflour, or a combination of the two. Pastry cream has a thicker

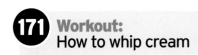

171 Workout:
How to whip cream

When preparing to whip cream, make sure that the cream, the mixing bowl, and all the utensils are chilled and the equipment is completely clean.

1 To stop the bowl from moving around, twist a towel into a ring and place the bowl on top.
2 Grip the bowl firmly in one hand and whip the cream with a whisk with the other.
3 Continue to whip the cream until it increases in volume by two or three times, forming soft peaks.

170 Workout: Making custard

Custard is any liquid thickened by the coagulation of egg yolks, and it can be stirred or baked. The stirred variety results in a soft, rich creamy sauce, while the baked kind results in a firm texture that can be sliced.

Recipe (yield: 6 cups/1.3 liters)
• 5 cups (1.1 liters) whole milk
• 1 vanilla pod
• 10 egg yolks
• 10 oz (300 g) sugar

Combine the milk and vanilla pod in a pan and bring to a boil, being careful not to burn it. In a separate bowl whisk the eggs and sugar together, then pour over the boiling liquid and whisk together. Cook over a low heat until the custard reaches 185°F (85°C). As soon as the custard coats the back of the spoon, take it off the heat and strain into a clean bowl. Serve or chill.

3

consistency than vanilla custard sauce, and with the addition of the starch it can be boiled. You need to boil it to achieve the right thickness and also to cook out the flour texture. Pastry creams are usually flavored with liquors, fruit extracts, or chocolate and used as a filling for pastries such as chocolate éclairs, cream puffs, or fruit tarts. Pastry cream, with the addition of whipped cream, can produce a mousseline (light mousse).

Creams

Creams (crèmes) include desserts such as Bavarian cream and blancmange. Bavarian cream (bavarois) is made by adding gelatin to custard before folding in whipped cream. You can then pour it into individual molds, or into one large mold, then chill it until it is firm, and serve it with fruit or fruit coulis (puréed fruit sauce). A classic dessert, using sponge fingers to line the mold first, then pouring in the Bavarian cream, is called a Charlotte Russe. Chiffon is similar to a Bavarian cream, but you use whipped egg whites instead of whipped cream, which you can then use as a pie filling.

Mousse

The word "mousse" simply means "froth," "foam," or "light." Mousse is similar to a Bavarian cream, but with the addition of whipped cream or whipped egg whites, or sometimes both. The air bubbles from the beaten egg whites or cream are trapped in the dessert base and provide the airy, almost spongelike, soft texture and velvety mouth-feel. Mousses are usually too soft to mold unless you add a small amount of gelatin to thicken them. Add melted chocolate if you want to make a classic chocolate mousse (see page 119). A mousse can be used on its own or as a filling for cakes or pastries.

Ice cream

Ice cream is custard that has been churned during freezing, to produce a silky smooth, rich texture. An endless variety of flavors can be added to the ice cream while churning. These include liqueurs, fruits, chocolate, nuts, and extracts of all kinds.

Commercial ice creams are required by the United States Food and Drug Administration to contain no less than 10 percent butterfat and at least 20 percent milk solids with no fat (MSNFs). A good-quality ice cream will have 40 percent solids and up to 50 percent overrun.

Gelato is an Italian ice cream made with milk. It is denser than normal ice cream because less air is incorporated during the churning process. It may or may not include eggs.

Frozen yogurt uses yogurt as a base, with the addition of milk or cream to add richness and smoothness. Sorbet does not contain dairy product and is made by mixing sugar, water, and flavoring before churning. Sherbet is fruit-based and made with milk or cream and churned to a light, grainy texture.

172 Workout: How to make a quenelle

A quenelle is a small oval ball shape that can be used to garnish sweet and savory items. To be able to quenelle quickly and effortlessly really shows off your culinary skills. The best thing to practice on is ice cream, because you can easily rectify your mistakes.

1 Take two matching spoons, fill one with ice cream and press the other on top. Press down and pull one spoon away from the other.

2 Repeat with the other spoon, scraping off any excess ice cream. It will take about three to four turns of the spoon to complete.

3 Repeat the process until you have a smooth, oval ball shape. Then place it on a plate and freeze until needed.

173 Workout: Making ice cream

Ice cream is custard that is churned during freezing and can be flavored with an endless variety of fruits, nuts, extracts, and liqueurs. The hallmark of a good ice cream is its smoothness and richness.

Recipe (yield: 6 cups/1.3 liters)
• 3 cups (750 ml) whole milk
• 1 cup (250 ml) heavy cream
• 1 vanilla pod
• 8 egg yolks
• 10 oz (300 g) sugar

Combine milk, cream, and vanilla pod in a pan and bring to a boil. In a separate bowl whisk eggs and sugar together, then pour over the boiling liquid and whisk. Cook over low heat until the custard reaches 180°F–185°F (82°C–85°C). Strain into a clean bowl. Chill in an ice bath, then churn in an ice-cream machine or place in the freezer and whisk every 30 minutes until frozen.

A word of caution

Whether you are making custards, fillings, creams, mousses, or ice creams, strict observance of all sanitation rules is essential because of the danger of bacterial contamination. Make sure you wash and sanitize all equipment before use. Taste with tasting spoons rather than your fingers while making. Chill as rapidly as possible if you are not serving the dish hot or warm. When chilled keep refrigerated at all times.

Resources

Top Culinary Schools

The Art Institutes International LLC

(888) 624-0300
www.artinstitutes.edu
The International Culinary Schools at The Art Institutes is North America's largest system of culinary programs offered at over 35 Art Institutes schools. You'll explore the world of international cuisines and use ingredients and techniques from around the globe.

The Culinary Institute of America

1946 Campus Drive
Hyde Park, NY 12538-1499
(800) CULINARY or 845-452-9430
www.ciachef.edu
If you see yourself as a chef, restaurateur, food writer, or food service manager, baker, pastry chef, or cake decorator, then the CIA in Hyde Park, New York, may be the school for you.

Johnson & Wales University (JWU)

8 Abbott Park Place
Providence, RI 02903
(401) 598-1000
www.jwu.edu
With campuses in Providence, Rhode Island, Charlotte, North Carolina, Miami, Florida, and Denver, Colorado, JWU offers two culinary degrees in four years: an Associate in Science (AS) degree after the first two years and a Bachelor of Science (BS) degree after the second two years.

Kendall College School of Culinary Arts

900 N. North Branch Street
Chicago, IL 60642
(888) 905-3632
www.kendall.edu
With instructors that have strong managerial experience, formal culinary training, and at least ten years' experience in industry, this college offers a variety of degrees and certificates in the culinary arts.

Le Cordon Bleu College of Culinary Arts

2895 Greenspoint Parkway
Hoffman Estates, IL 60169
www.chefs.edu
The culinary arts programs of this college draw upon over a 100-year heritage of culinary excellence, representing classic culinary techniques with modern innovations and the latest in global cuisine.

Professional bodies and training organizations

American Culinary Federation (ACF)

180 Center Place Way
St. Augustine, FL 32095
(800) 624-9458
www.acfchefs.org
Largest professional chefs' organization in the United States since 1929.

The International Council on Hotel Restaurant and Institutional Education (CHRIE)

2810 North Parham Road, Suite 230
Richmond, VA 23294
(804) 346-4800
www.chrie.org

International Association of Culinary Professionals (IACP)

304 West Liberty Street, Suite 201
Louisville, KY 40202
(502) 581-9786
www.iacp.com

The James Beard Foundation

167 West 12th Street
New York, NY 10011
(212) 675-4984
www.jamesbeard.org

National Restaurant Association (NRA)

1200 17th Street, NW
Washington, DC 20036
(202) 331-5900
www.restaurant.org

Research Chefs Association (RCA)

1100 Johnson Ferry Road, Suite 300
Atlanta, GA 30342
(404) 252-3663
www.culinology.com
Association of chefs and food scientists.

Slow Food USA

20 Jay Street, M04
Brooklyn, NY 11201
(718) 260-8000
www.slowfoodusa.org

World Association of Chefs' Societies (WACS)

www.wacs2000.org
International body of 72 official chefs associations.

Women Chefs and Restaurateurs (WCR)

P.O. Box 1875
Madison, AL 35758
(877) 927-7787
www.womenchefs.org

Magazines and journals

Art Culinaire
Bon Appétit
Caterer and Hotelkeeper
Chef
Chocolatier
Cooking Light
Cook's Illustrated
Culinary Trends
Eating Well
Food and Wine

Glossary

A la carte *(alla kart)*
A menu on which each food and beverage item is listed and priced separately. Foods are cooked to order as opposed to foods cooked in advance and held for later use.

Acid
A substance that neutralizes a base (alkaline) in a liquid solution. Lemon juice, vinegar, and wine are commonly used culinary acids.

Aerate
To incorporate air into a mixture through sifting, mixing, or whisking.

Albumen
The white of the egg, which makes up about 70 percent of the egg and contains the highest proportion of protein.

Amino acid
The basic molecular component of proteins, which are made up of oxygen, hydrogen, carbon, and nitrogen atoms: the building blocks of protein. Of the 20 amino acids in the human diet, nine are called "essential" because they cannot be produced by the body and must be supplied through the diet.

Anaerobic bacteria
Bacteria that live without the presence of oxygen.

Appetizer
First course to a meal, usually light, small portions of hot or cold foods.

Aromatic
An ingredient added to enhance the natural aromas of a dish. Aromatics include flavorings, such as herbs and spices.

Au gratin *(oh GRAH-tan)*
Foods with a brown or crusted top through the use of a broiler or salamander.

Bacteria
Single-celled microscopic organisms, some of which can cause disease, while others have beneficial properties.

Bain marie *(ban ma-REE)*
The French term for a hot-water bath that cooks or keeps food hot. A container that holds food in a hot-water bath.

Baked blind
An unfilled pastry shell that is made using baking beans to support the crust as it bakes.

Baking
A dry-heat method of cooking in which the food is surrounded by hot air, as in an oven.

Barding
The use of thin slices of fat to cover meats or poultry in order to protect, keep moist, and self-baste during cooking.

Baste
To moisten foods during cooking with melted fat or by dripping a sauce or liquid to prevent drying and to add flavor.

Béarnaise *(bare-NAYZ)*
A sauce made from egg yolks and warm butter and flavored with a reduction of vinegar, shallots, and peppercorns, finished with tarragon and chervil.

Béchamel *(bay-shah-mell)*
A sauce made by thickening milk with a white roux.

Beurre blanc *(burr BLAHNK)*
French for white butter. A classic emulsified butter sauce made from shallots, white wine, and butter.

Beurre manié *(burr man-YAY)*
"Kneaded butter." Equal amounts of butter and flour by weight combined and whisked into a simmering sauce to thicken and add sheen and flavor.

Bisque (bisk)
A soup made from shellfish and classically thickened with rice.

Bivalves
Mollusks such as clams, scallops, oysters, and mussels that have two bilateral shells attached at a central hinge.

Blanching
Briefly and partially cooking a food in boiling water or hot fat.

Boiling
A moist-heat cooking method that uses convection to transfer heat from hot liquid to a food (approximately 212°F/100°C).

Bouquet garni *(boo-KAY gar-NEE)*
A small bundle of fresh herbs tied together to flavor stocks, sauces, soups, and stews.

Braise
A combination cooking method in which foods are first browned in hot fat, then covered and slowly cooked in a small amount of liquid.

Breading
A coating of breadcrumbs, cornmeal, or other dry meal applied to foods to be deep-fried or pan-fried. The process of applying the coating.

Broiling
A dry-heat method of cooking in which foods are cooked by heat radiating from an overhead element.

Calorie
A unit of energy measured by the amount of heat to raise 1,000 grams of water by 1°C.

Caramelization
The process of cooking sugars. The browning of sugar enhances the flavor and appearance of food. The caramelization of sugar occurs at 320°F-360°F (160°C- 182°C).

Carbohydrate
A group of compounds composed of oxygen, hydrogen, and carbon that supply the body with energy (four calories per gram); carbohydrates are classified as simple (sugars) and complex (starches).

Clarification
The process of removing impurities from a liquid. The process of transforming a broth into a clear soup such as a consommé.

Coagulation of protein
The irreversible transformation of proteins from liquid or semi-liquid state to a solid state by the application of heat.

Collagen
A fibrous protein found in animal connective tissue that is converted into gelatin when cooked with moisture over a long period.

Combination cooking
Cooking methods, principally braising and stewing, which employ both dry- and moist-heat procedures.

Conching
Stirring melted chocolate with large stones or metal rollers to create a smooth texture in the finished chocolate.

Conduction
The transfer of heat from one item to another through direct contact, a pot or pan, oven racks, or grill rods.

Convection
The transfer of heat caused by the natural movement of molecules in a fluid (whether air, water, or fat) from a warmer area to a cooler one; mechanical convection is the movement of molecules caused by stirring.

Cooking medium
The air, fat, water, or steam in which a food is cooked.

Crustaceans
Shellfish characterized by a hard outer skeleton or shell, such as lobsters, crayfish, crabs, and shrimp.

Curdling
The separation of milk or egg mixtures into solid and liquid components. Caused by high heat, overcooking, or the presence of acids.

Deep-frying
A dry-heat method of cooking that uses convection to transfer heat to a food submerged in hot fat. Foods are often covered with bread crumbs or batter before being cooked.

Deglaze
To dissolve cooked particles remaining on the bottom of a roasting tray or saucepan with a liquid such as water, wine, or stock, which is used as the base of a sauce.

Dry-heat cooking methods
Cooking methods—broiling, grilling, roasting, baking, sautéeing, pan-frying—and deep frying—that use air or fat to transfer heat through conduction and convection; dry-heat cooking methods allow surface sugars to caramelize.

Emulsification
The process by which unmixable liquids such as oil and water are forced into a uniform distribution, as when making mayonnaise.

Emulsion
A uniform mixture of two or more unmixable liquids; emulsions can be temporary, permanent, or semi-permanent.

Entrée
The main dish of a menu, usually meat, poultry, fish, or shellfish, served with vegetables and a starch.

Fabricate
To cut a large portion of raw meat, poultry, or fish into smaller portions or cuts.

Fat
A group of compounds composed of oxygen, hydrogen, and carbon atoms that supply the body with energy (nine calories per gram); fats are classified as saturated, monounsaturated, or polyunsaturated. The general term for butter, lard, shortening, oil, and margarine; used as cooking media or ingredients.

Fermentation
The process by which yeast converts sugar into alcohol and carbon dioxide and the time that dough is left to rise.

Fiber
Indigestible cellulose found in grains, fruits, and vegetables, that aids digestion. Also referred to as roughage.

Frying
Dry-heat cooking method in which foods are cooked in hot fat; includes sautéeing, stir-frying, pan-frying, and deep-frying.

Game
Animals and birds hunted for sport or food.

Gastronomy
The art and science of eating well.

Gourmet
A connoisseur of fine food and drink.

Grill
A dry-heat method of cooking in which foods are cooked by heat radiating from a source located below a cooking element. Also the piece of equipment on which grilling takes place.

HACCP
Hazard Analysis Critical Control Points. Standards and controls established for time and temperature, and safe handling practices.

Hollandaise (ohll-uhn-daze)
A classic emulsified sauce made of warm melted butter, egg yolks, and flavorings.

Infuse
To flavor a liquid by steeping it with ingredients such as herbs, spices, tea, or coffee.

IQF
Individually quick-frozen—individual food items frozen rapidly.

Irradiation
A preservation method used for certain fruits, vegetables, grains, spices, meats, and poultry in which ionizing radiation sterilizes the food, slows ripening, and prevents sprouting.

Lard
Inserting thin pieces of fat into low-fat meats to add moisture while roasting or braising.

Leavener
An ingredient or process that produces or incorporates gases in a baked product to increase volume and provide structure and texture. Can be chemical (baking powder) or mechanical (folding in air in whipped egg whites or cream) or biological (yeast).

Liaison (lee-yeh-zon)
Mixture of egg yolks and cream used to thicken and enrich sauces.

Maillard reaction
The process whereby sugar breaks down in the presence of protein.

Marbling
Streaks of fat within meat that makes it tender and juicy.

Marinate
To soak food in a seasoned liquid to add flavor and tenderize. Liquid marinades are usually based on wine or vinegar, dry marinades are usually salt-based.

Microwave cooking
Heating method that uses radiation to cook food by agitating water molecules, creating friction and heat, which spreads through the food by conduction and convection.

Mirepoix (meer-pwa)
Chopped onions, carrots, and celery added to flavor stocks, stews, and other foods, generally in the proportion of 50 percent onions, 25 percent carrots, and 25 percent celery, by weight.

Mise en place (meez on plahs)
French for "putting everything in place"—getting ingredients and equipment ready for use.

Moist-heat cooking methods
Cooking methods—simmering, poaching, boiling, and steaming—that use water or steam to transfer heat. Moist-heat cooking methods are used to emphasize the natural flavors of foods.

Molecular gastronomy
Investigation into the chemistry and physics behind the preparation of food.

Mollusk
Shellfish with hard outer shells and no internal skeleton. Mollusks also include gastropods, bivalves, and cephalopods. Examples are clams, oysters, snails, octopus, and squid.

Nutrients
The chemical substances found in food that nourish the body by promoting growth, facilitating body functions, and providing energy. There are six categories of nutrients: proteins, carbohydrates, fats, water, minerals, and vitamins.

Oil
Fat that stays liquid at room temperature.

Pan-broiling
Dry-heat cooking method that uses conduction to transfer heat to food.

Pan-frying
A dry-heat cooking method in which food is cooked in a moderate amount of fat.

Par-boiling
Partially cooking a food in boiling or simmering liquid.

Par-cooking
Partially cooking a food by any cooking method.

Pasteurization
The process of heating a food item to a certain temperature, for a specific period of time, to kill bacteria.

Pathogen
Any organism that causes disease usually refers to bacteria. 95 percent of all food-borne illnesses are from pathogens.

Poaching
A moist-heat cooking method that uses convection to transfer heat through submergence in a liquid (approximately 160ºF-180ºF/ 71ºC-82ºC).

Proteins
A group of compounds composed of oxygen, hydrogen, carbon, and nitrogen atoms necessary for manufacturing, maintaining, and repairing body tissue, and as an alternative source of energy. Protein chains are constructed of various combinations of amino acids. Proteins can be obtained from both animal and vegetable sources.

Quenelle (kuh-nehl)
Small oval-shaped portion of food, made using two spoons. Also a lightly poached dumpling made from a forcemeat.

Roast
A dry-heat method of cooking food that surrounds it with hot air in an enclosed environment or on a spit over an open fire.

Salamander
A small broiler used for glazing and browning the tops of food.

Saturated fats
Fats found mainly in animal products such as meat, milk, butter, and eggs. These fats tend to be solid at room temperature and are primarily of animal origin. Coconut oil, palm oil, and cocoa butter are vegetable sources of saturated fat.

Sautéeing (saw-tay-ing)
A dry-heat cooking method that uses conduction to transfer heat from a hot pan to food with the aid of a small amount of fat at a high temperature.

Season
To enhance flavor by adding salt, pepper, herbs, and spices. To age food, usually beef or game. To prepare a pot or pan to prevent sticking when cooking.

Shallow-poaching
A moist-heating cooking method that combines poaching and steaming. The liquid is often used as the base of a sauce.

Shocking
To chill blanched or par-cooked foods in iced water to halt the cooking process.

Simmering
A moist-heat cooking method that uses convection to transfer heat from a hot liquid by submersion (approximately 185ºF-205ºF/85ºC-96ºC).

Smoke point
The temperature at which a fat begins to break down and smoke.

Sous-vide (soo-veed)
Cooking by vacuum-sealed pouches in a low-temperature water bath.

Starch
Complex carbohydrates from plants, rice, grains, pasta, or potatoes.

Steam
A moist-heat cooking method in which heat is transferred by contact with steam.

Stew
A slow-cooked dish, often incorporating small pieces of meat that have been blanched or browned, then cooked in a small amount of liquid, and served in the sauce.

Stir-frying
A dry-heat method of cooking in which foods are cooked in a small amount of fat at a very high temperature and stirred constantly while cooking.

Sweat
To cook without coloring over a low heat to soften the food item and to release the flavor of the item.

Temper
To heat gently and gradually without curdling.

Temperature danger zone
The temperature range in which bacteria multiply rapidly: 41ºF-135ºF (5ºC-57ºC).

Tempering
To melt chocolate, keeping it smooth and glossy or slowly raising the temperature of a cold liquid.

Thickening agents
Food ingredients that thicken sauces or liquids—flour and butter, arrowroot or gelatin, and liaisons.

Vegan (VEE-gun)
A vegetarian who does not eat any foods derived from animals.

Vegetarian
A person who does not eat meat, poultry, fish, or shellfish.

Zest
The outer rind of citrus fruit, which contains the oil, flavor, and aroma.

Index

Acknowledgments

Author acknowledgments

A book is not just the work of one person, but the work of a number of very talented people, so I'd like to take this opportunity to thank Kate Kirby for giving me the opportunity to write this. This has been a dream come true—thank you for your patience, enthusiasm, support, and vision.

I would like to thank Jo Godfrey Wood, Cathy Meeus, and Hugh Schermuly for their patience, consistency, expertise, design, and professionalism with this book. It has been a pleasure to get to know them and work with them, even with 5,000 miles separating us.

I would also like to thank my faculty and students who helped with this project, namely Bryan Hudson, Sara Jumper, Michael Shaw, Andres Chaparro, Paul McVety, Karl Guggenmos, Patti DelBello, and Wanda Cropper. This book would not have been possible without their guidance, assistance, and support.

Most of all I would like to thank my wife, Alison, and my sons Jonathan, Matthew, and James, for their love, support, and understanding while my attention was diverted from family matters to endless hours in front of a computer while writing this book.

Publisher acknowledgments

Quarto would like to thank the following for kindly supplying images for inclusion in this book:
p.2 Photolibrary.com/freshfoodimages/Chris L Jones
p.7 Getty Images/Brian Doben
p.11 Photolibrary.com/Ticket/Yadid Levy
p.92 Getty Images/David Prince

iStock
Shutterstock

Specially commissioned photography by Simon Pask

While every effort has been made to credit contributors, Quarto would like to apologize should there have been any omissions or errors, and would be pleased to make the appropriate correction for future editions of the book.